Somebody's Got My Robe

JOHN YARRINGTON

Abingdon Press
Nashville

SOMEBODY'S GOT MY ROBE

Copyright © 1997 by Abingdon Press

This book is printed on recycled, acid-free, elemental chlorine-free paper.

Scripture quotations are from the New Revised Standard Version of the Bible, copyright © 1989 by the Division of Christian Education of the National Council of the Churches of Christ in the USA. Used by permission.

ISBN 0-687-12170-1

98 99 00 01 02 03 04 05 06—10 9 8 7 6 5 4 3 2

MANUFACTURED IN THE UNITED STATES OF AMERICA

Contents

INTRODUCTION

"There's a Choir in a Church Singing Weekly" (Weakly?)

(Sung to the tune of "The Church in the Wildwood")

1. There's a church with a choir singing weekly,
   they work so the product is good.
   Oftentimes when we look it's a different group
   than the ones who on Wednesday there stood.

   REFRAIN:
   O, Help! Help! Help! Help!
   Help us recruit and train them,
   those wonderful bright volunteers.
   Give us love and direction and patience
   as we toil through this valley of tears.

2. Now we know when they show for rehearsal
   Their heart's in the place that is right.
   But their tone, pitch, and rhythm is shaky,
   Giving rise to conductor fright!

3. When the pastor for hymns does the choosin',
   It could be a scary affair.
   Oftentimes at the text they are lookin',
   But the tune's unfamiliar or square.

4. Many times at the console is sitting
   A person with minimal skill.
   So for anthem or hymn or some psalmody,
   One's advised: Careful choice fills the bill.

5. Staff relations can be quite a hassle
   With schedules and trips and the like.
   When we feel that the choir takes a seat in back,
   We are tempted to just "take a hike."

6. Now the moral is clear: It's a hard job
   To be in the work of the church.
   So we meet here today for a fresh look
   For new wisdom we all do search!

This is a book about working with volunteer singers in church. It seeks to address two questions: (1) What do *they* need? (2) What do *I* need?

What Do They Need?
Whatever motivates, enlivens, encourages, satisfies and keeps them coming back.

What Do I Need?
Whatever I can do to stay alive, function, be enlivened, encouraged, satisfied—and keep coming back!

The title, "Somebody's Got My Robe," is a statement, usually delivered with some heat, to the director personally or to the assembled choir, lumping the guilty all together in one fell swoop. The companion statement is, "Somebody's got my hymnal." Relatively sane, well-adjusted folk, who function well in life, handle everything from birth to brain surgery with aplomb, turn into gibbering, insulting, angry children when confronted with an empty hook or slot. They are not easily appeased, gentle reader! I have seen these otherwise solid citizens actually grab a fellow choir member by the scruff of the robe collar, attempting to find out just who's "got their robe." As if, for one Sunday, one couldn't find another garment. To the statement: "Somebody's got my hymnal," I often respond: "Is it blue?" This seems to calm some. I have not, however, found a reasonable solution to the robe "crisis."

This phenomenon is symptomatic of the general clientele with which we work. In workshops, I often speak of choir types. Many of you can readily identify with these personalities:

- **The Ludens lady**. She has enough cough drops stuffed into her folder (in the side pockets, don't you know) to satisfy the entire choir.
- **The anal-retentive bass.** He always has a question. Sign on the board for the evening: "Come to Sanctuary." Question: "I don't have 'Come to Sanctuary' in my folder." (I do not make this stuff up!)
- **The questioner.** This individual looks at the agenda order of anthems for rehearsal: Item 3: "Bach Cantata." Question: "Is that Bach Cantata No. 4?" Answer: "No, you remember this is the Sunday we're doing four Bach cantatas, all with period instruments." (How many Bach cantatas do you have in your folder?)
- **The grumbler.** He comes early, makes comments loudly for the director to hear: Everything from, "Not *that* anthem again," to "We're just singing from the hymnal! I think I'll go home."
- **The latecomer.** She is always fifteen to thirty minutes late, no matter when the rehearsal starts. One evening, the entire choir stood and applauded when our latecomer finally arrived!
- **The body-language expert.** He sits with arms folded across his body. This is not the sign language for: "I'm sure glad you went to that church music workshop and came back with some new ideas and techniques."

Truly, when confronted with a new situation, one can spot these types (and others) and think: "I know you. I've seen you before."

So, for all of you who have patiently endured my puns, bulletin bloopers, orchestra jokes (in score order, of course) and have said, "You need to put all of this 'wisdom' and 'humor' in a book," this tome's for you!

CHAPTER ONE

What Do "They" Need?
Expectations of a Volunteer Choir Member

Bulletin Blooper
Sign on church billboard: "At the evening service tonight, the sermon topic will be 'What is Hell?' Come early and listen to our choir practice."

Let us begin with three important definitions:

Choir: A musical organization thought to have been invented by G. F. Handel to ensure the perpetuation of performances of Messiah.

Conductor: The person at the front of the orchestra or choir, with his (or her) back to the audience (usually out of embarrassment). His primary function is to imitate a windmill for the aesthetic effect. His chief weapon is the baton, which everyone is pretending to watch carefully. If the performance goes well, he takes all the credit; if badly, the performers get the blame.

Singer: A special type of musician, notable for the inability to count at all. Unlike other musicians, who must rely on the instrument to produce sound, singers use only the vocal apparatus (i.e., the voice). There are certain inherent advantages and disadvantages—a singer wishing to improve his or her technique cannot simply buy a better instrument. But then some of the carrying cases are so much more attractive. Singers are usually paid less than instrumentalists (if at all), and usually remain standing throughout the performance. Often, someone will faint.

As one who has spent a lifetime working with volunteer singers, I attribute some of my longevity to the ability to put myself in the place of those I conduct, anticipating their needs, being sensitive to their pain. Yarrington's law has always been: "What do they need?" So, here's a checklist:

CHALLENGE
HUMOR
OPPORTUNITY
INTEREST
REHEARSAL
SECURITY

The sharp-eyed observer will immediately notice that these six components spell out the word *choirs*. This may seem obvious, but I find the "obvious" not always so.

Example: Stack of music with sign reading: "Music for June 3"
Choir member's question: "Is this for June 3?"

Example (instruction): "Please hold your candle in your right hand, folders in your left hand."
Choir member's question: "Which hand does my folder go in?"

Example: Agenda for rehearsal on board—Sunday's anthems in red, marked with asterisk
Choir member's question: "What's for Sunday?"

Challenge

Volunteer choir members respond to a variety of styles with a level of difficulty from easy to more difficult. They may complain about the more difficult anthems or larger works, but usually come to appreciate what has taken more effort. Most can learn to mark their music and be responsible for attacks, releases, dynamics, awkward page turns (are there any other kind?). Some need lots of drill on any anthem before feeling comfortable. Generally, they will grow and develop from *more* challenge, not from less.

Humor

Laughter really is the best medicine. If we directors wouldn't take ourselves too seriously and turn the laughter toward the podium occasionally, what *is* serious would become easier to accomplish. The wise director takes cues from the troops. Often a remark from a choir member serves to change the prevailing mood. But if someone removes cough drops or Kleenex from a folder, or, perish the thought, if "somebody's got our robe," singers often do not find humor therein. What we are about is so very important and serious, that finding humor makes the task easier.

Opportunity

I often tell my choir after seeing them on Wednesday evenings, that they look as if they have had a week of Mondays! Nothing revives anyone quicker or is more therapeutic than singing. Most singers want to get better and will enjoy pertinent warm-ups as long as there is a lot of singing and not too much talking from the director. We directors are prone to talk too much—we should let the choir sing, demonstrate what we want, vary the routine, and keep encouraging them to get better. Almost everyone has visions of solos dancing on their vocal bands and directors should find opportunities for the appropriate use of as many as possible. Most resent the "prima donna" system employed in some situations. (Please see definition at the end of this chapter.) Volunteers get nervous, and need much rehearsal and reassurance if they are to "solo."

Interest

Our personal interest in "them" is the ministry part of the equation. I always try to put a personal note on any correspondence or bulletin that is duplicated. A pre- or post-rehearsal visit, a phone call, a written note, a hospital visit are meaningful. Everyone is busy, but all are needy and all need strokes. Your personal interest renews the dedication to get in the car and "come back" on Wednesday and Sunday.

Rehearsal

It is obvious to most when the director has done his or her homework. These folk in front of us have taken out an entire evening and need to feel a sense of accomplishment when finished. If routines for music distribution, folders, hymnals, robes are established, seating patterns defined, and the rehearsal area in order, there is a sense that all is well. The rehearsal plan should have good flow, pace, and timing. (See chapter 6 on rehearsal planning.) It is always better if the pace is fast (not furious) and if specific instructions for remedial work are given. "All right, let's do that again" seldom brings any result. Too much talking from the podium is the cardinal sin, bores everyone, and is counterproductive.

Security

Most directors work about six weeks ahead on anthems, hymns, and responses. Choir singers need to feel the comfort of repetition. When they miss rehearsal, it's nice to know that preparation is ongoing for more than this next Sunday. When they look up they should get clear indication of where and when to breathe, when to begin, when to stop. (See chapter 7, on conducting.) They need constant reminders about dynamics, phrase shape, accents, articulation, word-shapes. The conducting "they" need is not overdone or fancy. All that sweating, swaying, singing along, snapping of fingers, banging of feet, leaning over into "their territory" really doesn't get the job done anyway. Remember, directors: if you *sing* with your choir, you can't *hear* them. Clear downbeats, good releases, reminders in gesture assure singers that if they have done their part by coming regularly to rehearsal, marking their music, and concentrating, you, the conductor, will not fail them.

Coda

So there. That wasn't so bad, was it? Perhaps the choir members would like to compile a handbook listing their expectations of the director. One final definition:

Prima donna: The most important female role in an opera. This is, of course, largely a matter of opinion. By extension, the term has come to be applied to any singers who merely behave as if their's were the most important role; that is to say, everyone. Derived from an Italian phrase that may be roughly translated as "pain in the neck," although some have a lower opinion.

One thing is certain; we don't need prima donnas in the choir loft—or on the podium.

Definitions are adapted from David W. Barber, *A Musician's Dictionary* (Chicago: Contemporary Books, Inc., 1991).

CHAPTER TWO

What Do I Need?
Musical/Pastoral Skill

Bulletin Blooper
"Don't let worry kill you—let the church help."

What do I need to keep myself fresh, alive, responsive, striving? How do I "keep coming back," issuing new challenges, attempting to teach unfamiliar hymns, changing the worship order, fighting all the dance/football/baseball/soccer/school schedules so that what is done in church might have the same careful preparation (rehearsal, practice) the "world" shows?

As is already obvious, I find much humor in working with people in church. It's my way of dealing with stress. As a matter of fact, if I should list four attributes of "need" for myself and others, they would be: (1) Commitment to the task, (2) constant skill level improvement, (3) humor, and (4) hospitality.

Here are some helpful (?) hints for church musicians to get things started:
- It is easier with a large choir.
- It is easier in a big church.
- Charisma and magic are helpful.
- You need only know music, not psychology.
- Telling them will always bring results. Example: "Sopranos, you are flat."
- Generally, people want to know and experience new hymns, new anthems, new ways.
- You can always depend on the adults to act their age.
- Humor is unimportant—work, work, work!
- Only "good" music and "good" hymns should be done. It is up to "us" to raise the standards.
- Organists should always play on every verse of every hymn—*sempre legato* and *fortississimo.*
- Always take yourself very seriously—after all, this is sacred music.

- Never sing from the balcony, aisles, or in the congregation. Always sing from the choir "loft."
- Remember, your problems are unique and much greater than others'. Here are some of your problems:
    - An unappreciative minister
    - Not enough money (for music, or for you)
    - A youth director who takes the kids away when you need them
    - Cantankerous soloists
    - Cantankerous congregational members
- Practice your catch phrases:
    - "Blend, blend, blend."
    - "Phrase, phrase."
    - "Support."
    - "All right, let's do that again." (Be sure not to be specific about what is to be done again.)
    - "Watch me." (For what?)

Always leave the impression that you know what these catch phrases mean. Create an aura of knowledge and mystery. But, by all means, never be too clear. The choir might really do what you ask—then what would you do?

Commitment

For me, another word for commitment is *community*. Somehow I must always remember that those who voluntarily come (whether children, youth, or adult) need from me a committed, constant presence. Leadership has its price. It is certainly easier to get into—and stay firmly entrenched in—the rut of doing the same things over and over, being careful to try to satisfy everyone in choir and congregation alike, practicing the art of accommodation to the point that we prostitute what we believe and become unhappy and even cynical. How many of us have colleagues who simply couldn't "take it" any more? The conflict between their musical and theological training and what they were expected or asked to do to fulfill and keep their jobs simply became too much.

The church growth writers would have us believe that we must embrace a consumer mentality in music and worship, offering the equivalent of "things go better with Coke" in a religious context. That the church should reach out to the unchurched gets no argument from me. That the church should be aware of and even embrace the most contemporary of marketing, computer, and advertising skills to promote its "product" may prove helpful. But I also believe that we need to be "in the world" not "of the world." We are in danger of losing our wonderful classical tradition of hymns and anthems in the name of "reaching" everyone. Balance is one thing, consumerism another. This is a tough time for trained musicians in anyone's local church.

All the more reason, gentle reader, for continually nurturing that element of our work that does bring satisfaction to us and to those with whom we work: *community.*

In an article in the *Christian Science Monitor,* Robert Shaw has this to say about *community:*

> A major part of life is spent looking for community. The fact that people can reach the extraordinary intellectual precocity of great music, and experience its beauty and ethical integrity by singing together with 50 or 100 other people, that's an extraordinary thing.

> The physical act of singing undoubtedly delights people. They find themselves expressing things they couldn't express by themselves soloistically. Everyone realizes you are doing something that is unavailable to you as an individual . . . singing together with the quality of literature now available brings everybody a delight in community without any loss of individuality and self-respect. You're doing something that only ennobles everybody.[1]

For me, commitment to community means rubbing shoulders and minds with the best, the most creative, the highest standards of musical craft and theological sensibility—not mucking around with whatever happens to be out on the street. This also means I must maintain my sense of what is most important, I must stay healthy physically and emotionally, and I must learn, somehow, that it is not necessary for me to sacrifice "me" for the equation of care + training + psychology + skill = community and an adequate level of performance without apology.

Writing in a communiqué from Yale Music School, John Bailey says:

I also learned what community was about, that people to make music together must love one another, or try to love one another. And I began to see that the musical community is in a sense a paradigm for other communities where love is operative.

My discovery at Drew was the freedom to say, "Your gift is really as a musician and you don't have to apologize for that; you've got to be you and you've got to pursue that and become one with that, not with what someone tells you a church musician has to be." [2]

Skill

What does "constant skill level improvement" mean? For me, it means a continual search for new information to enliven my teaching. Sometimes we don't question others because they might find out that we don't know everything we ought to know. I find that really successful people in our field are usually delighted to talk with me, answer questions, and even to come and work with our groups here at the church. In addition, I think it is important to keep up by reading and attending seminars and workshops. While I can't "be" someone else, I can see and learn what works and adapt it to my situation and my personality.

The chapters in this book dealing specifically with techniques and philosophy in working with choirs and instrumentalists attempt to distill much experience into some practical ways of working. Much of it has been gleaned from others. So many of you have said to me at workshops, "You have been in my rehearsals." I have been there and am there and I believe that we can "come back again" refreshed and renewed, but only if we are willing to constantly assess our strengths and weaknesses and to work on our own improvement.

I find it helpful to always have a big project: a major score to study (even if I am not going to conduct it), a book about style or music history or theory that I plow through to prove to myself that all brain cells are not dead yet, a seminar like the one sponsored by the Carnegie Hall Foundation in New York or numerous others where I have to dig to stay up. Otherwise, I slowly but surely sink back to the level of the ordinary and accept less than I should from myself or others.

Find a colleague you trust and admire and keep a dialogue going about where you are in your journey of music and of faith. I have a friend I call frequently, never identifying myself, simply starting the conversation and he does likewise. We lift each other up when the day-to-day "stuff" of our existence threatens to undo us. We speak freely, cynically, humorously, and yes, gentle reader, we talk about our choir members and our ministers, relieving stress and getting our heads straight so we can "come back" for some more. We always discuss literature, concepts, warm-ups and bounce ideas off each other. I am grateful for this friendship.

Humor

In speaking about this book to my choir members, I have threatened to publish their names and use them as examples. I have said to them: "None of you is innocent—sue me!" Grady Nutt said, "Laughter is God's hand on the shoulder of a troubled world." I believe that the road becomes smoother when we are able to laugh at ourselves and laugh with others. My friend, the Rev. Charles Foster Johnson, Senior Pastor of Second Baptist Church in Lubbock, Texas, writing in the church's newsletter, *The Second Page*, speaks about "laughter as a spiritual gift":

Perhaps we had better start taking laughter more seriously. Doctors are beginning to see that laughter has healing power. Several years ago in his book, *Anatomy of an Illness*, Norman Cousins reported that laughter played a strategic role in his recovery from a deadly disease. It seems that laughter is a kind of mental and physical exercise, what one writer calls "internal jogging" that helps relax our tensions and relieve our stress. One physician insists that if our daily intake of laughter is less than 15 laughs—including 3 belly laughs—we are "under-laughed."[3]

Pastor Johnson continues:

God knew all of this already. The Great Physician writes us a prescription we all need: "A cheerful heart is a good medicine, but a downcast spirit dries up the bones" (Prov. 17:22). It is a great grace to laugh. Nothing can warm and bless a community of faith more quickly than corporate laughter. No question that worship should be conducted with a sense of reverence and dignity, but joy should be present too wherever the name of the Lord is celebrated. Maybe the "laughing revivals" presently conducted in the Pentecostal and charismatic churches isn't such a bad idea for the rest of us. One can certainly think of worse things for a church to do than laugh.[4]

Hospitality

When that congregational member comes up to you, eyes blazing, after the second worship service (you've been there since 6:00 A.M., setting up chairs, putting out hymnals, putting out fires, teaching Sunday school, attending to last minute details) and asks: "Can the organist play *softer*?" my answer is: "Yes." You might as well stop with that because you're not going to win that argument. Richard Avery and Donald Marsh used to say that the negative voice gets heard, which is the religious equivalent of the squeaky wheel. People seem to feel free to voice their discontent to church staffers without resorting to common courtesy or timing. I don't know about you, but *how* I am approached, and *when* I am approached make all the difference. I find it helpful to listen to what the congregation tells me and pay heed, but I am not a doormat and, often, I have good reasons for choosing what is done.

If I am able to create a hospitable atmosphere for myself and others, I am less likely to become defensive and say something I later regret. The corollary is that I expect the same of others. No one can be "served" every Sunday. If we try to do that we run the risk of not "serving" anyone. Paul Westermeyer speaks of this in a later chapter. This means that much is allowed in the name of worship and music, always done with skill, practice and integrity, and what speaks to one turns another off. Each must exist together and allow freedom for the other.

What does it mean to be hospitable? Let me turn to Henri J. M. Nouwen from *The Wounded Healer*:

> Hospitality is the virtue which allows us to break through the narrowness of our own fears and to open our houses to the stranger, with the intuition that salvation comes to us in the form of a tired traveler. Hospitality makes anxious disciples into powerful witnesses, makes suspicious owners into generous givers, and makes closed-minded sectarians into interested recipients of new ideas and insights. But it has become very difficult for us today to fully understand the implications of hospitality. Like the Semite nomads, we live in a desert

17

with many lonely travelers who are looking for a moment of peace, for a fresh drink and for a sign of encouragement so they can continue their mysterious search for freedom.

What does hospitality as a healing power require? It requires first of all that the host feel at home in his own house and secondly, that he(she) create a free and fearless place for the unexpected visitor. Therefore, hospitality embraces two concepts: concentration and community. [5]

I believe that part of our job is to constantly encourage, work for, and insist on hospitality on the part of ourselves and others. Nothing is so injurious as one who simply cannot accept another's needs and wants expressed, particularly in music, in ways absolutely foreign and even distasteful to that one. We express our disagreement in love and back it up with something more than a long-held prejudice, and we *allow* others to have "their day." As teachers (choir directors) we can do much to create this "hospitality" in rehearsal. In an article in *The Christian Century*, Dr. Parker J. Palmer identifies a style of teaching embracing the concept of hospitality:

To teach is, first, to create a space in which a meeting can occur, a meeting between those who seek truth and the truth which seeks them. . . . The teacher must help create a community within that space, a network of relationships between the learners and the subject at hand. Such a community begins with a teacher who has a living, personal relationship with the subject at hand, it grows as students sense that they are invited to forget their own living relationships with the teacher, the subject, and each other.

Hospitality is the primary quality a learning community must have—the sense that all parties to the relationship are respected, taken seriously, affirmed. The reason for hospitable community in the classroom is not to make learning painless, but to make painful things possible. Such things as the exposure of ignorance, the testing of tentative ideas, the mutual criticism of thought—all those things that make knowledge more than individual opinion, things so essential to learning that are all but impossible in a combative academic environment.

Consensus does not mean a democracy of opinion in which a majority vote equals truth. Consensus is, rather, a process of inquiry in which the truth that emerges through listening and responding to each other and the subject at hand is more likely to transcend collective opinion than to fall prey to it. [6]

I approach my work, my planning, my decision in a attitude of hospitality. I recognize that when I have the responsibility of choice (in hymns, liturgy, anthems, and so on), I also have the obligation to serve many needs, which may mean choosing material not particularly appealing to me but serving the needs of the community. It means being in touch with who is being served, getting out and about, teaching Sunday school, leading singing at church events, making myself available in a posture of love, which often carries the day when nothing else will.

Is there tension involved in this stance? You bet there is! Am I constantly discouraged because the hospitality extended to others does not come back my way? You bet I am! When I commit to the task, using humor in a positive way, practice and perfect my skills as a musician, pastor, and teacher and remember that the best atmosphere in school or church is that of hospitality, I am on the road to a music ministry that challenges as well as serves—one with the highest standards of quality and expectation. And I don't have to choose between ministry and music—I can have them both!

Notes

1. Robert Shaw in *Christian Science Monitor* (March 13, 1996): 3.

2. John Bailey in *Institute of Sacred Music Newsletter,* Yale University, May 1977.

3. Charles Foster Johnson in *The Second Page,* newsletter of Second Baptist Church, Lubbock, Texas, October 10, 1995.

4. Ibid.

5. Henri J. M. Nouwen, *The Wounded Healer: Ministry in a Contemporary Society* (New York: Doubleday, 1979), pp. 12-13.

6. Parker J. Palmer in *The Christian Century* (October 21, 1981): 1051-35.

CHAPTER THREE

Somebody's Got My Robe!

A Philosophy of This Work

Another title might be: "Music in Ministry: Commitment to Community." This is the philosophy out of which the rest of the book proceeds. I always pose two questions regarding the "practice" of church music:

1. Do musical standards (demands) need to be sacrificed in the name of ministry?
2. Do ministry demands (concerns) need to be sacrificed in the name of musical standards (demands)?

Volunteer choir singers are those wonderful folk who "volunteer" to come to rehearsal week in and week out, without whom there would be no music ministry. Surely no one disagrees with this. However, gentle reader, these folk also "volunteer" wrong pitches and rhythms, "volunteer" to miss rehearsal but show up on Sunday, dedicated but unrehearsed (which is not the same as unwashed, but close), and "volunteer" their opinions on a wide range of musical subjects, mainly your choice of anthems, service music, and hymns.

Since 1965, I have been in full-time service through the church's music. I have attempted musical performances with all age groups, working for beautiful vowel sounds, crisp consonants, singing in tune with appropriate balance, joined occasionally by a solo instrument, a small ensemble, or full orchestra. Always, I have attempted to choose what was "appropriate" to the occasion or the season and to provide challenge for myself and the singers.

So where's the rub? It has been my experience that the more one works on the elements of what I call "choral hygiene" (vowels, consonants, musicality, form, and so on), the more one expects commitment to regular rehearsal attendance, the more one challenges the best "performance" possible, the more one is open to the notion that this is an "ego trip" and has nothing to do with church music. It's as if the phrase, "that's pretty good for a church choir" is the operative phrase. The "product" doesn't matter, only the intent.

The tension for me, all these years, has been to satisfy the demands of musical experience while not sacrificing the needs of ministry. In other words, if I expect good "performance" out of children, youth, or adults, does that mean I don't care about them personally? I think not. What it does mean is that I cannot justify bad singing, bad playing, or poor preparation in the name of some misguided idea of "ministry."

Paul Westermeyer, in a wonderful article in *The Christian Century*, gives perspective:

> Church musicians are all too typically regarded as those who sustain the church by providing musical services. This view has them responsible for creating fellowship and good feeling in the congregation—dispensing services that keep everybody happy, entertain the troops and give everybody warm fuzzies.

> This job description creates two intolerable tensions. First, if a congregation is even in the remotest sense Christian and not totally a reflection of the culture, its church musicians feel the gnawing sense that simply meeting people's needs is wrong. The second tension comes from the pressure of trying to satisfy the desires of everybody in the congregation. It can be difficult to try to meet what are often competing demands: some people want gospel hymns, some want rock, some want Lutheran chorales, still others don't want to sing at all and expect the choir to do it. Some want the choir to sing sixteenth-century motets, others want to sing only nineteenth-century music. One group wants nonsexist texts when referring to humanity; others want nonsexist terms for both humanity and God; others insist one should never alter the original text. The musician is supposed to meet all those requests.

> Defined this way, the life of a church musician is a nightmare indeed. Ultimately, what Stanley Hauerwas and William Willimon refer to as the "voracious appetites" of demanding people can devour the musician. So, to avoid being devoured, musicians seek to manipulate

tastes and needs. Some use commercial television as a model . . . others push for high taste or for their personal tastes. These approaches inevitably lead to frustration because they focus on power. The musicians' work gets reduced either to obvious power plays and outright war or to subtle forms of control, which are the antithesis of freedom.[1]

What is the role, then, of church musicians? They are fundamentally responsible for the people's song, the church's song. Church musicians are the chief singers, the leaders of the church's song. They are responsible for singing the congregation's whole story.

Westermeyer speaks of the importance of Sunday morning worship, the church year, planning, practice, and relationships. The only way to sing the fullness of the Christian story, he says, is over many Sunday mornings. Since we are all tempted to sing only our favorite parts of the story, we need some way to protect the people and to protect us from ourselves. The church year gives us that way.

He also maintains that the musician must practice:

Not to practice is to regard the people with contempt. Musicians must practice far ahead so things are ready when they need to be, and they must practice up to the last moment so that they will be fresh for the service.

Underneath all this is the church musicians' relationship with parishioners and with God. Because church musicians operate within a community of grace that is sustained by God, they do not have to try to manipulate people or their tastes. The musician is free to take risks, to fail and to succeed, because sustenance is not the musicians' concern; faithfully singing the song with the people is. That means knowing the big story, knowing the people's stories and their capacities, and then serving them with care.[2]

In coming across the person of Dr. Harold Best, and in reading his wonderful book, *Music Through the Eyes of Faith*, I have found some peace and solace, some accommodation with the tensions of music versus ministry. This is a work steeped in scripture, out of which a philosophy of music making in the church proceeds.

Music doesn't just happen; it has to be made, worked out. Sometimes this working out is spontaneous, other times greatly labored and time consuming. But, in any case, questions like these come to mind: Why can we make music and how do so many people go about making it in so many ways? Is making music like making other things? What is creativity itself? Where does creativity come from? Creativity, says the good Doctor, is the ability to imagine something—think it up—and then execute it or make it.

The quality of the crafting will be determined by the degree of technique and skill the maker possesses. Technique and skill are closely connected: technique is the facilitator and skill is the degree and refinement of the facility. Yet creativity, technique, and skill often get mixed up with each other in the musical world. If I am creative, I imagine a different way of music making than someone else would. I must then possess the skill to execute this difference. If I can only duplicate someone else's music making, I am not creative but merely skillful. If my imitation of someone else is third-rate, then neither skill nor creativity is apparent.

What does this mean to our creativity and music making? Above all, it means that we should not make music in order to prove that we are or to authenticate ourselves. God created in us the capability for understanding that we are authenticated in him, not in what we do. In the final analysis, music making is neither a means nor an end but an offering, therefore an act of worship. All music makers everywhere must understand this and proceed accordingly. Nothing but harm lies ahead if we try to authenticate ourselves with our musical works or become so attached to them—addicted might be a better word—that we have no sense of worth or being without this "proof" of our existence. . . . our union with God, both in our createdness and our redemption, is the only authenticity worth claiming. And our music making must continually bear witness to that.

The creation is the best example for the complete integration of worth and function. Everything that God creates has intrinsic worth, and everything that has worth functions. Any serious discussion of music making is bound to include the subject of function or functionalism. . . . institutionalized settings for art—concerts, exhibits, museums, and theaters—are virtually considered separate places, supposedly free of the kind of functionalism found in the outside world. At the same time, functionalists maintain that music and the rest of the arts do not have to be so isolated and singularly perceived. According to them, the arts should be useful, near at hand, and at work with other activities.[3]

I do not wish to do disservice to Dr. Best's carefully reasoned, beautifully written work. I encourage the reading of it in its entirety. When he speaks of the issue of function and worth, he touches on the tension I expressed earlier between the demands of music and of ministry. Those in our profession who only do "the best," the "highest," and look down on any other offering, do great harm, in my opinion. Those who overlook artistic quality and worth in order to obtain results do similar harm.

Says Dr. Best:

The lesson for music makers, especially Christians, is obvious. We should not merely "grind it out" because we know that "it's just for prayer meeting" or subvert quality and integrity in the interest of "communication." We must always remember that the very subversion of quality communicates something about the kind of gospel we are trying to propagate. If we faithfully followed God's example, there would no longer be the crassness and cynicism of the throwaway or the false pomp and pretense of art for the ages. Nor would the Holy Spirit be continually pestered to turn poor work into blessed work. The Christian musician has no right whatsoever to assume that anything other than the mind of Christ and the Creatorhood of God should guide every note composed, arranged, played and sung. This is nothing other than good stewardship. The reason is simple: God the Creator has made it clear that function and worth, usefulness and integrity, are to be joined in every action.

Each musician must come to experience the dignity, rightness, and eventual joy of putting things aside, of emptying oneself and taking the form of a servant. Such musicians must be able to move back and forth, gracefully, servingly, and willingly, from the symphony to the folk tune; back and forth without complaint, compromise, or snobbery, without the conceit that doing an oratorio is somehow more worthy or more deserving than doing a hymn tune. All servant musicians must be able to be in creative transit, serving this community and challenging that one, all the while showing grace, power, elegance, and imagination.[4]

Roger McMurrin, formerly Director of Music at the Highland Park Presbyterian Church in Dallas, Texas, once said: "Some church choir directors program for their colleagues." His comment has stuck with me through the years and I believe he is right in his observation. Why do those of us who are trained in music (sometimes in theology) feel that we cannot "move back and forth gracefully, servingly and willingly?" Is it because we in truth authenticate ourselves by the music we make and we are afraid that if we dare to sing "gospel" hymns, when appropriate, even "contemporary" gospel hymns, or anything outside the pale of Bach-Beethoven-Mozart or their twentieth-century equivalents, our colleagues will think less of us?

> A part of this problem is that we see music prostituted in the name of "bringing in the gospel." We cannot help but judge a poorly constructed product, an out-of-tune rendition, or one of those sing-along-with-the-tape (you "interact" with the tape don't you know) productions. We are not satisfied that the "product" is justified in the name of intention. We know that, to survive, we have to live in the land of functionalism and of art. One without the other simply won't work. "When the sole purpose of music and art is to perpetuate familiarity, be a tool of the gospel, or preserve the 'right' conditions for worship, with no room for artistic vision or change . . . many honest church musicians are either pressured to compromise or forced out of the practice itself."[5]

We must, I believe, dwell in the land of hospitality and servanthood, with careful, appropriate choice, sufficient practice, and high expectation. We could do ourselves a favor by speaking about the "familiar" and the "unfamiliar" instead of "new" and "old" or worse, "good" and "bad." The idea that "we" are going to raise someone's standards usually results in only raising his or her hackles. When we give people the idea that they are somehow not up to "musical snuff" and that we will give them what they need and what we deem appropriate or "good," we create not understanding or good will, but bad will and hostility.

Does this mean that we "allow" anything in the name of ministry? Does this mean that if someone wants a song for a wedding or a funeral or suggests something for worship service that we are obligated to use it? Do we never take a stand for what we believe? Of course we have to take a stand, but the way in which we offer alternatives ("that song would be wonderful at the reception") and deal with people pastorally makes all the difference. The attitude can always be one of offering help to make appropriate choices instead of a pejorative, snobbish, demeaning treatment that leaves people feeling stupid, tasteless, and not very cultured for wanting a certain kind of music.

> To empty ourselves the way Christ did is to remain the same all the while. This means that integrity, conscience, imagination, worth, and excellence are to be as evident in the tune as in the symphony. The lessons of simplicity and complexity, worth and usefulness, variety and unity, familiarity and strangeness, function and quality are all driven by the larger lesson of the emptying in the Incarnation. The servant musician, living this way, is finally learning the lesson of artistic wisdom. He or she is learning to acquire the gift of functional integrity, which is nothing other than the ability to maintain excellence, high purpose, and artfulness in the fulfillment of any creative task in any context to which God voices a call. [6]

Notes
1. Paul Westermeyer, "The Practical Life of the Church Musician" in *The Christian Century* (September 1989).

2. Ibid.

3. Harold Best, *Music Through the Eyes of Faith* (San Francisco: Harper, 1993), pp. 12-16.

4. Ibid., pp. 30, 33.

5. Ibid., p. 29.

6. Ibid., pp. 33-34.

CHAPTER FOUR

Putting Carts Before Horses
Vocal Health

Bulletin Blooper

Wednesday the ladies liturgy will meet. Mrs. Johnson will sing "Put Me in My Little Bed," accompanied by the pastor.

There I was, a guest clinician, facing a church choir in another state for a weekend workshop. Said the director: "Do you want me to warm them up?" Thinking I would learn from watching and listening, I agreed.

What ensued was probably pretty typical in many rehearsal rooms around the country. Beginning in C major, the choir sang lustily, heavily, and "out-of-tunely" that age-old vocal studio exercise "Mah-May-Mee-Moh-Moo" in a arpeggiated pattern of 1-3-5-3-1, ascending ever higher by half steps. I decided this was the vocal equivalent of a Jane Fonda workout tape, but with nothing like the results.

Aren't we supposed to "warm up" our groups, gentle reader? Don't the vocalises we learned from Madame Slavianski in her studio work just fine for a group? Shouldn't we start where people are comfortable (C major) and ascend by half steps?

Let's be clear: no orchestra or band comes onstage, sits down, and plays. First they all blow, bow, or clang, then they tune up—*then* they play. Listening is as much a part of the warm-up as the playing itself. When we start with our groups in a low key, singing loudly and heavily and move up by half steps, we are beginning in absolutely the wrong way, for we engage the heavy or speaking-voice mechanism at the outset and, by singing loudly, we do not encourage listening.

A five-minute warm-up and tune-up says, "We now come together as a group—an ensemble—to review the basics of posture and tall vowel sounds and immediately apply what we are learning to the literature of the moment. It is 'Christian' to sound good, to sing in tune with proper blend and balance, using well-formed vowel sounds and to allow the words we sing to flow through us to those who hear." This worthy goal cannot be accomplished without technique.

As a private voice teacher who works with young voices in high school, I spend a good bit of time helping my students find the part of their voice that is not the speaking part. Where we speak is the most developed since it is the most used. What does this mean? It means I start from midvoice and work down, using lots of breath, singing lightly with good posture—singing "on the breath."

What William Vennard calls the "yawn-sigh" ("an exercise in dynamic registration") requires students to take a breath with released jaw, and slide in a descending pattern of about five notes on "yah."

The same principle is espoused by that great guru of children's choirs, Helen Kemp, with a fire siren, a "yoo-hoo" chant, a noon whistle, or a European ambulance sound: all of these partake *first* of a light mechanism or "head voice" sound coming *down*—not going *up!*

I'm convinced that much of the out-of-tune singing in church choirs, particularly in the men's section (mostly in the basses) comes from heavy, "chesty," lower mechanism production. All the more reason for starting in midvoice, working lightly, encouraging listening and tone connected to the breath, and gradually increasing both volume and range.

No rehearsal should start, in my opinion, without some stretching, relaxing of shoulders, and bobbing (gently) of heads. Singing is physical and anything we do to enhance what Ann Jones calls "body attitude" (not posture) works to our advantage.

Many do not warm up because they feel it is a waste of time. If warm-ups are attempted, they are often too complicated and have little or no application to the music to be sung. One could get up every day for a year and sing "mah, may, mee, moh, moo" like a magic incantation, but nothing vocally productive would happen. One would be better off with simple exercises that lead immediately into application. Developing a sound-in-the-room as a frame of reference is preferable to "mah-ing" or "mee-ing" while scurrying up and down the scale in a meaningless effort. The results will be gradual, but building on a solid foundation will produce long-term results. We are tempted to forego the basics in a rush to learn new anthems and prepare programs, but sooner or later we must deal with "how it sounds."

The title of this chapter is derived from three articles in the *Choral Journal* (February, March, and April of 1983), by Dr. Leon Thurman, with whom I have worked. Thurman is a vocal specialist with much experience in vocal dysfunction. I hope not to do a disservice to the amount of material in these articles by excerpting some of it and would strongly encourage contacting the American Choral Directors Association office in Lawton, Oklahoma for back copies of these three articles.

> In rehearsals and performances we choral conductors want to hear musical results: accurate pitches, precise timing, clear diction, expressive phrasing, authentic style, and good choral tone. The most fundamental cause of intonation problems is not a "bad ear"; it is underdeveloped vocal coordination. The most fundamental cause of imprecise timing is not a poor timing sense; it is underdeveloped vocal agility. The most fundamental cause of "sloppy" diction is not laziness; it is either underdeveloped or overdeveloped articulatory skill. Overly effortful, interfering vocal coordination is also the most fundamental cause of poor choral tone and inexpressive singing.

> The musical skills which we all want to hear are absolutely necessary. The mountaintop, peak experiences that send us into that altered state of consciousness which words dare not describe, cannot be fully known without them. But all of those elements of expressive choral performance are either realized or inhibited by the way individual voices sound them.

> Yet as a profession, we choral conductors are least trained and least knowledgeable in voice use and care. Our typical training leads us to believe that 8 to 10 years of choir singing, 2 to 4 years of private voice lessons, one or two courses in choral conducting or methods, and possibly a semester of vocal pedagogy will give us all we need to know about voices. So, many of us stop learning. Choral conductor education is concerned predominantly with rehearsal procedure and musicianship—choral pedagogy. Our rehearsals and performances, therefore, are concerned more often with the musical results than with what gets us there—voices. THE CART IS BEFORE THE HORSE.[1]

Thurman says that developing musicianship skills in our singers before teaching them how to use their voices well, "would be like a football coach teaching defensive strategy before teaching how to tackle; or a sewing teacher teaching quilt design before teaching how to use a needle and thread." He also states that "writing about what makes voices tick is risky. Abbreviated hints about teaching energetic but healthy voice skills, the vocal physiology involved and its aerodynamic and acoustic effects, risk being imprecise and will be oversimplified to those who are acquainted with the science of voice." Thurman hopes that the information in these three articles will whet appetites for deeper knowledge.

Vocal production is *all* below the level of conscious control. You can't reach down and "finger" an A—you can't make those vocal bands (they are not "cords" and do not function like the strings of a violin!) really do anything by touching them. You can't go to the music store and "buy" your vocal instrument—*you* are the instrument. So, we are all left with the psychology of vocal development. The more we know about the vocal physiology, the better we can develop imagery and exercise to enhance individual voice development. In a choir, we must not, we cannot, ignore this important vocal development. This means we must tailor what we do to the group, always being careful to ensure individual development and growth.

Howard Swan has said: "Sometimes the choral director cloaks his own ignorance of the singing mechanism by dealing directly with the interpretive elements in a score and thus avoids any approach to the vocal problems of the individuals in his chorus." A survey by Jeter indicated that beginning vocal teachers identified the teaching of vocal techniques as a significant difficulty in their first year of teaching.

Says Thurman:

Our strong desire to hear musical qualities in rehearsal and performance sometimes leads us to ignore the signs of vocal abuse in our singers—hoarseness, for instance. Many of us are so taken by public performance that we feel we must sing often and devote almost all of our rehearsal time to performance preparation. There is not time, then, for warm-ups or for teaching the very skills which can enable healthy, expressive performance—vocal skills. We tend to discuss voice in the context of "choral tone" or "sound." We often utilize methods of achieving a congregate tonal effect more than methods which enable our singers to explore, discover, and develop their individual vocal potentials and appropriate contribution to choral tone.[2]

Thurman maintains that the primary functions of the human larynx are not the production of speech and song but relate to survival:

> For instance, the vocal folds go into spasm when any foreign matter approaches them, thus protecting the delicate tissues of the lungs. Noise making is a survival function—frightening away potential predators, maintaining emotional equilibrium through moaning or crying, for instance—but these are not nearly as extensive a use of voice as speech and song. Language and its use in singing evolved in a social context as the human nervous system developed the capacity to process sounded symbols.

> Singers are vocal athletes. Those who use their voices to an extent which is beyond occasional, quiet conversation are engaging in athletic voice use. Singing, teaching, acting, and other athletic uses of the human noise-maker are specialized, strenuous functions which have been imposed on the larynx, for which it was not primarily intended. Careful conditioning, training, and hygienic care are necessary, therefore, if the owner is to use it well over a life span.[3]

The following could well be a credo for all of us: "The goal of good voice skill teaching is to enhance the potential for beautiful healthy voice use by our singers throughout life by: (1) teaching them how to preserve voice health, therefore availability for optimal use; and (2) teaching them how to speak and sing with an appropriate balance of physical/mental freedom and energy."

If we begin from the top (or middle range), unhinge the jaw, and get the tone "on the breath," we are a long way toward the kind of energetic, tuneful, healthy singing of which Dr. Thurman speaks. Taken together, these three elements spell the word *TUB:*

> **T**   Begin from the **T**op (lighter mechanism).
> **U**   **U**nhinge the jaw.
> **B**   Get the tone connected to the **B**reath.

When the choir comes together, a careful, five-minute warm-up/tune-up serves many purposes:

1. It focuses the group on the task. We don't just start singing "something" anymore than a good orchestra just starts playing.

2. We help everyone adjust their "body attitude," first by stretching and limbering up, then by using their stance to breathe correctly, with a cold air breath, and sing with good follow-through. When we ask for a "cold air" breath, for instance, we encourage a raised palate and give space for tone and resonance. "Feel cold air in the back of your mouth" is a clear direction.

3. The "yawn-sigh" mentioned earlier is similar to a yawn *without a yawny tone*. We should always talk about releasing the jaw, raising the upper jaw, and beginning as a follow-through to our breath. No breath should ever be taken, then held. The taking of breath implies completion in sound. Breathy is better than a forced, effortful start.

4. We develop vocal agility and flexibility in our singers by asking for light, energetic, often *staccato*, singing. Later in the chapter you will see suggested exercises for this and other purposes.

5. We encourage listening and tuning. This means more careful listening and less heavy "unthinking" singing. This does not mean unenergetic, nonfocused tone. It does mean lots of energy directed into less effortful production. It also means that, as we warm up, we ask for more sound and for more range, but only after a careful, thoughtful beginning.

6. Your voice is the best model. Talking to them is often nonproductive. Model for your choir not only the sound but also the inflection, color, mood, and resonance you desire. After you model, listen to what they do. Positive reinforcement works the best. "Sopranos: you're flat" may solve *your* frustration, but really doesn't help *them* sing a bit better!

7. The warm-up/tune-up period needs to be simple. With a couple of exceptions I don't ever recommend buying one of those choral exercise books because, for the most part, the suggested exercises are too complicated. We want our people to focus on good body attitude, with relaxed (released) jaws, singing on-the-breath with beauty and clarity. As Allen Pote is wont to say, let's use the K.I.S.S. method: KEEP IT SIMPLE, STUPID.

8. The warm-up/tune-up should be thought out and written down. It should also be varied. Doing the same three or four exercises every time becomes routine and monotonous. Look for spots in hymns or anthems that might be excerpted for your use. Have fun! Your choir will love singing "Flexibility" from *Sing Legato* by Dr. Kenneth Jennings.

After this five-minute period, starting with something well known is a good idea. Even a new anthem that doesn't make great demands of range or dynamics could be started, singing on neutral syllables, but we don't preserve the "vocal gold" of which Robert Shaw speaks if we "holler" immediately after warming up.

I was in a rehearsal in another state, directed by a well-known clinician, who began warming up in C major, much as described at the beginning of this chapter. No one paid much attention to *how* they were singing or *what* it sounded like. After this painful period, work commenced on one of the Handel "Coronation" anthems. For the rest of the rehearsal, the singing was effortful, under pitch, and increasingly frustrating to the singers who really didn't have any idea *why*. The conductor, also increasingly frustrated, talked more and more about musical ideas, articulation, style, nuance, all of which are extremely important, but the *beginning* of the rehearsal doomed the rest of the effort. This need not be so!

Warm-up/Tune-up/Build the Sound

Those of us who work with (and depend on) volunteer singers must always seek to establish the best vocal concepts for them individually, and for the group as a whole. I believe in a five-minute warm-up/tune-up/shape-up time to begin the rehearsal—*no matter what!* When I think I am saving time by eliminating this valuable step, almost always I am proved wrong.

Why is this? Isn't singing just a "natural," beautiful, effortless expression arising out of a need/love to make wonderful sounds by oneself and with a group? Don't all of us have fond memories of our around-the-campfire experiences, where we "crooned a toon" with that indescribable aura of fellowship and goodwill? Don't we just open our mouths, coordinate our breath, and "let fly"?

No, gentle reader. Singing is a *learned* function. Breathing is a learned function. Coordination of sound and breath is a learned function. In our groups we encounter such a variety of vocal types that we must get everyone more or less on the same page. Thus, what we do in our first five minutes with our singers sets us up for the entire evening. We usually encounter:

- High chest breathing
- Little coordination with the taking of breath and emitting of sound
- Jaws tight, tongues tense, bodies stressed
- Regionalism in vowel production
- Lack of sight-reading ability
- Forced, on-the-vocal-bands sound—edgy, unsupported, nasal, ugly

The challenge is not to throw up your hands (or simply throw up) but to dig in and be the best voice teacher you can be. Here are some considerations:

What works in a private voice session (exercises, approaches, and so on) does not always work in a group setting. However, the basics always apply (remember the "TUB" method):

The Basics
Start from the **T**op.
             Unhinge the jaw.
Connect the **B**reath.

Tall, vowel sounds with raised soft palate, "released" jaw (not "dropped"), and energetic breath connected to the sound, always bring results.

Asking those present to roll their shoulders, stretch, bend over gently, drop the head down and back (not roll it around), yawn, sigh—even the tried and true "turn and give your neighbor a backrub" is important. We *are* the instrument. Volunteer singers, especially, come from daily stress and strain and this physical limbering up is one of the best things we can do for them.

Sally Herman suggests the following:

You might begin by having everyone close their eyes, place all ten fingers of their hands on their thighs, and make sure all ten toes are touching the floor. Now concentrate on sending all tension in the body out the ends of the fingers and toes.[4]

We start from the top (or lighter mechanism, if you will) because our speaking range usually is the strongest. In young singers, of course, that so-called "chest sound" (heavy mechanism) has to be connected with the upper register, or we are doomed to a small range and corresponding music with little challenge.

The secret of a balanced attack is the synchronization of breath pressure with the closure of the glottis. In a tight attack, the bands are closed first and then pressure is applied. In a breathy attack, the breath is flowing out before the bands start to close. In a balanced or soft attack, the breath and the bands arrive simultaneously starting the sound cleanly, without any evidence of strains or wasted breath.

Imagining that the tone starts in the head instead of larynx or throat may help direct attention away from the throat. Stressing the idea of maintaining the beginning-of-a-yawn position while singing can be helpful because of the relaxation it creates and because it tends to put the larynx in its best position for singing.[5]

We unhinge the jaw because a tight or inflexible position of the jaw is at the root of many vocal problems. Combine this with tension at the root of the tongue, and the singer can produce some pretty awful, constricted sounds.

We connect the breath because it is the life source for good singing and because so many young singers utilize a high chest approach. Taking a breath implies completion in a sound, similar, I tell my students, to a windup before batting. "Stroke-of-the-glottis" is the correct term for the approximation of sound with breath. A forced sound, one that is too loud, too soft, raspy, or harsh, is not what we want from our singers. We also talk about making a good vocal "attack":

A good attack must be prepared physically as well as mentally. A perfect attack occurs when the breath support mechanism and the vocal bands are brought into action simultaneously and efficiently, without unnecessary tension or wasted breath.

Practice starting good sounds by using this routine:
1. Breathe in as if beginning a yawn.
2. Feel your body expand around the middle.
3. Suspend your breath just as you are comfortably full of air.
4. Start the sound by merely thinking to do so, without conscious physical effort.[6]

If we are serious about improving the vocal sounds of our groups and enhancing the experience of each individual singer, we must be serious about the approach taken in the warm-up and in each subsequent anthem or hymn. So many times, in my experience, vocal problems, bad intonation, and sloppy rhythm can be helped by a vocal approach to the problem. Your voice is still your best model. Sing to your group with the best possible tone, inflection, color, and nuance whatever you wish. Listen to their response. Sing again. Encourage them, be positive. Don't *talk* to them, *sing* to them.

My dad is eighty-one and lives in Heber Spring, Arkansas. Many years ago, he sang in a choir I directed in Tulsa. After the first rehearsal, these pearls of wisdom spewed forth: "Don't talk! We didn't come to hear you talk! We came to sing!" I have followed that valuable advice all these years. We choral directors talk too much! We explain too much! Brief is always better. If I have really thought through what I hope will happen from the warm-up throughout the entire rehearsal; if I have timed the rehearsal and have been honest in my appraisal of how long something may take; if I move swiftly, clearly, cleanly, and train singers to get to the right page, measure, and so on, then and only then do I have the chance for a successful rehearsal. It doesn't always work and sometimes "they" don't cooperate, but if you plan your work (as Helen Kemp always says) and then analyze, not rationalize, you are on the road.

Collections

After having advised you, gentle reader, not to buy collections of warm-ups because often they are much too complicated, let me suggest three I live by:

Sing Legato by Kenneth Jennings (Neil A. Kjos V74A). Accompaniment edition. These are wonderful. They treat basic kinds of musical articulations: *legato, staccato,* and *marcato*. Some assist in the development of good tone, some deal with intervals, and so on. The words do the teaching ("Sing legato, sing smoothly, flowing from note to note").

Choral Warm-ups for Minds, Ears, and Voices by Leonard Van Camp (Lawson-Gould). Solid approach to what has been discussed above. Van Camp suggests that the entire sequence can be executed in about seven minutes. Once the routines are learned the singers will not need music and will be able to concentrate on thinking, listening, and singing. The written instructions to the singers are what a director would say to them if he or she were teaching the warm-ups by rote. Although these exercises have been written with the mixed choir in mind, they can be easily and effectively adapted for all-male or all-female groups.

The Complete Choral Warm-up Book, Robinson/Althouse (Alfred 11653). I know, I know, this is a terrible title. However, I commend the volume to you. It is concise, helpful, and the layout is wonderful: explanation on the left, exercise on the right. I refer constantly to this for help and for variety.

Variety

One last time: there are those who do the same exercises every time and they maintain that this solves all problems. Most of the literature I read says to vary the "routine." Why? Because what we get used to, we take for granted, and effectiveness suffers. So much of good singing with amateur groups is mental anyway, so we should always be on our toes to challenge this aspect of their work. The only way that happens is to vary what is done. The important consideration is that we must know what we hope to accomplish and the sequence and flow need careful planning and attention.

The Warm-up

1. Always begin by stretching, limbering up, reaching for the ceiling, bending over gently, rolling shoulders. Be careful to let the head fall forward and back; don't roll it around.

2. Sometimes it is helpful to ask everyone to turn and knead the shoulders of their neighbor, then turn in the opposite direction and repeat the process.

Start From the Top

Ask everyone to sigh, use plenty of "s," start from the middle of their voice, lightly, and slide the sound down. E♭ major with a B♭ on top is a good starting place. Remember that beginning in a lower key, C major, for instance, and going up is the worst way to begin. It encourages lower-register production (speaking voice) and gets the rehearsal off to a shouty, heavy start. Begin on B♭ and sing a four-note major descending scale on "sigh."

Ex. (SssssAH————ee)

Encourage breath connection (even breathiness) and a relaxed jaw. Help singers understand that their follow-through is crucial. A breath taken, then held, seldom results in the sound we want.

Ask them to make a gesture across their body (a sweeping gesture) in conjunction with the beginning sound. (Adults hate this but it really works for them; it is easier with children!)

Repeat, moving the starting pitch up a half step. (Don't go below octave C below middle C and encourage "the lower the lighter."

Cool Air Breath

Almost everyone agrees that a raised soft palate is essential to good tone. Taking a "cool air breath" (a Bev Henson phrase) lifts that palate and raises the uvula. Singing on that sensation helps resonance and tone. Noiseless breath is important. A relaxed (released) jaw is also important.

Speaking for Resonance

Sometimes a spoken phrase such as OH ⌝↓ NO ⌝↓ YAHM ⌝↓ , HELL-O (beginning in midvoice and singing over the top into the next register), or I LOVE ⌝↓ TO SING ⌝↓ , followed by a descending five-note scale is effective for breath coordination and resonance. Beginning singers who have trouble getting into a register other than their speaking voice can demonstrate for themselves the possibility of more range and resonance.

Resonance Bringers

While we know that there really isn't any sound up there in that part of our head, sometimes called the "mask" by voice teachers, we certainly feel the sensation of vibration in the cheekbones, and the sounds "m," "n," and "ng" accentuate that sensation. If we are careful to lift the soft palate with cool air we will not get a resulting nasal production, but one that efficiently uses breath flow for tone. Breathiness is, after all, a faulty approximation of the vocal folds. Resonance bringers help. Remember also that most of what we are talking about has to be overdone, and repeated, and overdone, and repeated. (Get the picture?) Bev Henson, my teacher, still has the best phrase for all of this: "If you are tired of hearing me say this (whatever it was), think how tired I am of saying it."

All the more reason, gentle reader, for varying the routine.

Falsetto

The Bee Gees have helped us considerably because falsetto is "in." That sensation of a fire siren or whistle on a "oo" vowel, beginning in midvoice and sliding up into falsetto is very helpful to reduce that effortful, strident sound we so often hear.

An exercise I have used a good bit has all the men beginning in falsetto, altos coming in second, sopranos third as follows:

All voices sing on "oo," *legato.*

Using Hymns

Certain hymns work well as we attempt to get our people to start from their head voice:

- "Come, Thou Almighty King" (begin in E♭ major, use only the first line and encourage energetic, light attack—from the top!)
- "Come, Christians, Join to Sing"
- "All Creatures of Our God and King" (the Alleluia section)

Using Anthems

Find particular sections in well-known anthems that may be extracted for warm-up purposes.

Unhinge the Jaw

Calling again on Dr. McKinney:

> The lower jaw must be free from tension and ready to move as needed if it is to function well as an articulator. Many of the muscles used in chewing and swallowing are attached to the lower jaw. It is very important that these muscles not be kept in a state of tension while you are singing; if they are tight, the throat will be tight, and the resulting sound will be tight.
>
> Many people have a hard time learning to relax the muscles which pull the jaw up and close the mouth. It is necessary to use these muscles to keep the mouth from hanging open as you perform your daily tasks: this means that these muscles must be kept under tension during all the hours you are awake, for some people truly relax them only when they go to sleep. If the muscles which raise the jaws are relaxed, the jaw will drop freely down. This is why the mouth often drops open when a person falls asleep. You should cultivate the feeling that your jaw is dropping open freely of its own weight while you are articulating. [7]

Again, beginning in E♭ major on a B♭, ask singers to slide the sound down on "yahm," releasing the jaw. Sometimes, they can place their fingers beside their ears (one on each side) and feel the jaw displacement. The important instruction is release, not drop. We are attempting to help them release tension, not create more by attempting something physical like dropping the jaw.

Cultivating a loose feeling (even slack) in the jaw and overdoing the effect will bring results. Descending five-note scales follow, with a "yahm" on each one, gently, in pitch. Sometimes a "yahm" slide, followed by a five-note descending scale is helpful. Singers are notorious for singing effortlessly on a "yahm" slide, following it up by the most effortful production possible as they sustain pitch. "Blah" is also helpful in a descending five-note pattern, again emphasizing relaxation and an overdone quality. "Bomb" is another useful word in this regard.

One of my favorite exercises is found in a little collection called *Canons, Songs and Blessings: A Kemp Family Collection* (Choristers Guild CGC-27).

Yup,* yup, yup, yup, yup dee yup dee yup dee aye. Tra -

la, la, la, la, la, la, la, la, la, la, la, la. Tra - la, la, la. Tra - la! *Hey!*

*yup = rhymes with foot

This exercise is also good for tongue articulation:

Because the tongue has to move for so many different sounds, it is important for it to have a resting place to return to—a point of reference. Vennard makes an analogy between this aspect of tongue position and the best defensive position of a tennis player. Players in a number of different sports employ reference points to enable them to repeat certain actions with a minimum of effort and a maximum of accuracy. This is the purpose of locating a resting place for the tongue.

For most singers the best point of reference seems to be the gum ridge just below the lower teeth. When you are singing any vowel the tip of the tongue should rest lightly on the gum ridge with the body of the tongue making the needed adjustments for a particular vowel. The tip will leave the point of reference to make various consonants, but should return to it quickly.[8]

Connect the Breath

One of the most helpful little exercises is found in a wonderful volume called *Children Sing His Praise*, edited by Donald Rotermund and published by Concordia. Chapter 5, written by Helen Kemp, is worth the price of the book because it embodies everything I've been talking about. Basic vocal technique must be taught, beginning with our children, or we don't have a prayer (tonally) for any improvement. Helen calls this exercise a "Consonant Caper."

A Consonant Caper with F, S, Sh

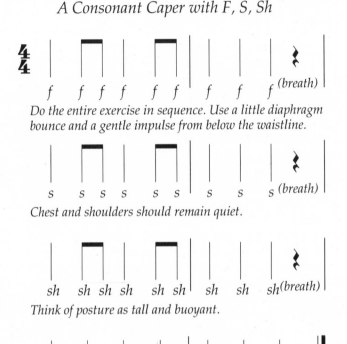

Do the entire exercise in sequence. Use a little diaphragm bounce and a gentle impulse from below the waistline.

Chest and shoulders should remain quiet.

Think of posture as tall and buoyant.

Singers crescendo to release all remaining breath as they bend over from the waist, relaxed and "dangley."

The tune "America" ("My Country 'Tis of Thee") is also good for breath energy and connection. Begin in F major and ask singers to sing *staccato* on "pahm" or "doot," singing every sound *staccato*—even the longer notes! *Staccato* singing on-the-breath is excellent for connecting and energizing the sound. It also reveals our sloppy intonation because we don't have time to "hang on" and "adjust" the pitch. Then sing *legato* on "loo" or "doo" and help singers follow through with their breath.

My original intention in this chapter was to write out various exercises I use, but I have decided to leave you to your own devices in that regard. It is easy to demonstrate some of these ideas in a workshop but harder to confine them to paper.

After the Warm-up: Where to Start?

After this careful warm-up/tune-up period, what follows should build on effortless, energetic singing in positive ways. We must listen to them. We are tempted to sing along, clap, snap, tap, and get ourselves so involved (see chapter 7 on conducting) that we really don't hear what is coming out. Honest listening in rehearsal is the prelude to improved singing and musicality.

Our job is to make musical sense out of what we do. Here is my checklist for that:

1. From the first, work for beauty of sound: tall vowels, crisp consonants, and so on. The idea that we can learn the notes, then put in expression, beauty, and tone is bunk.

2. Interest people in the beauty of the text—speak the text for word shapes, inflection, direction, destination—make sense of the text by dealing with thought and ideas (phrases).

3. Don't let your people be unmusical while they learn notes.

4. Form is a great teacher—help them see how the piece is constructed—locate sections or divisions, repeated places, patterns, and so on.

5. Encourage a wide range of dynamics—especially work to energize the soft singing.

6. Pencils are a necessary part of rehearsal—teach your people to mark their music. "I'll remember" is a well-worn statement from choir members. I tell them: "You won't even remember where your car is parked in the church lot—mark now please." And tell them what to mark: Circle difficult spots, underline important syllables, mark breath or no breath and places where you lift but do not breathe, draw arrows up for notes needing higher pitch, and down over important destination words making phrase sense. (See chapter 5 on style.)

7. The introduction to something "new" is often crucial to the project: the "establishing shot" means you know what the crucial elements are. From the beginning, interest them in the unique qualities of the piece. If it is the text, for instance, speak the text aloud, listening for word shapes, taking delight in sound as it fills your mouth. If the melody is central, work on a neutral syllable, not "notey" but always with a sense of phrase shape and destination. Remember, it takes more energy to ascend than to descend.

Anticipate trouble spots but be willing to take what you get "for free." Encourage, particularly in the initial stages of a new anthem or major work, an atmosphere of "hospitality." Hospitality doesn't make painful things (like change) less painful, only possible. (See discussion on hospitality in chapter 2.) We don't like change (remember the seven last words of the church: "We've never done it that way before") and adult choir members are often the least open, flexible, and hospitable. Everyone has a right to an opinion, but rudeness should not be tolerated. Almost every choir has at least one naysayer, but one learns how to deal with individuals positively and, in some cases, privately. The rehearsal is not, however, a free-for-all. The negative voice is always the strongest— and the most strident.

It's all worth it when a choir member comes up and says something like: "You know, I didn't like that Vaughan Williams anthem at first. But I've gradually grown to love it and appreciate the hard work."

As mentioned earlier, when one spends time on the craft of choral singing, the product or performance is much better than just trusting the Holy Spirit to do the work. I believe that out-of-tune, unintelligent, lackluster singing done in the name of the Lord is as much an affront as a poorly prepared (or delivered) sermon, mangled scripture, wandering, aimless prayers, and general inattention to what we do and how we do it. I have been known to say: "Sloppiness is not next to godliness."

So, where's the rub? There are always those who confuse our intention to bring the best we have to offer with a misguided sense of our own egos. I remember Dr. Best's injunction that I don't have to validate myself or my worth by the quality of the work or the judgment rendered on the tastes of others—colleagues or parishioners. I should not, however, justify bad performance in the name of ministry. My friend, the late Roger Deschner, has framed this discussion much better than anyone else I know:

An ill-thought-out cliché has been on the lips of many church musicians. They say our choirs do not "perform," nor do our organists, instrumentalists, and soloists. To them, performance is a bad word. "Performers" are people who act out parts (whether they believe it or not) for personal accolades. Although we are all tempted to play that part, it is the very opposite of what we are called to do in our tradition.

The problem is that "performance," at root, has never had that crass meaning. We need the word in talking about church music; God uses the word in making demands on our choirs. It must be salvaged. If we are talking about "selfish uses of church music," then that's what we should say, and that temptation to misuse church music must always be held to the light. But God asks us today in our choirs, as God has always asked, that we give. . . our best "performance," that which we have carefully prepared for God's use.

Performance simply means to complete what one has set out to do, to accomplish it with the special skills that are required. Performance asks us to take the time to complete thorough preparations for an anthem. Performance asks us to hone our skills so that a more perfect gift can be offered to God and our neighbor. Performance demands commitment, time, work, and a willingness to use our talents. The opposite of good performance is half-done, half-learned, misunderstood, shoddy, ragtag offerings of music in worship that too often afflict us and must embarrass even a caring, forgiving God. Shoddy offerings are signs of a lack of faith and commitment. Good performance arises out of our faith and love of God.[9]

BEAUTIFUL VOWEL SOUNDS
(with apologies to Stephen Foster)

Beau-ti-ful vowel sounds, soon there will be
Man-y rich voic-es in true har-mo-ny.
Glo-ry to God, whose truth waits for you,
Sing-ing tall vowel sounds with pitch clean and true.
(Isn't this fun so far?)

Tak-ing a cool breath, op-'ning your throat,
Start from your head voice and float, people, float!
Now is the time be-fore night is o'er,
Sing-ing good vowel sounds with feet on the floor.
(There's more!)

Con-son-ants cause the text to be clear. (no "r")
Don't be a-fraid to ar-tic-u-late here. (no "r")
Those in the mid-dle need much more care,
Bet-ter and bet-ter our mu-sic to share.
(The big finish!)

Some are el-i-ded: Let all be smart.
Some r's are not sung, like "here," "there," and "heart."
Some r's are flipped, like glo-ry (glow-dee) and praise (p'days)
Beau-ti-ful vowel sounds and con-son-ants raise! *(J.Y.)*

Dedicated to the Joyful Noise and Sanctuary Choirs
Pulaski Heights United Methodist Church
August 21, 1996

Notes

1. Leon Thurman, *Choral Journal* (February 1983): 5.
2. Leon Thurman, *Choral Journal* (March 1993): 5.
3. Ibid.
4. Sally Herman, *In Search of Musical Excellence* (Dayton, Ohio: Roger Dean Publishing Co., 1996), p. 9.
5. James C. McKinney, *The Diagnosis and Correction of Vocal Faults* (Nashville: Broadman, 1982), p. 93.
6. Ibid., p. 82.
7. Ibid., p. 155.
8. Helen Kemp, *Canons, Songs and Blessings: A Kemp Family Collection* (Garland, Tex.: Choristers Guild, 1990), p. 20.
9. Roger Deschner, *Your Ministry of Singing in the Church Choir* (Nashville: Discipleship Resources, 1990), pp. 13-15.

CHAPTER FIVE

In Your Easter Bonnet
What's in Style? What's in a Style?

<u>Bulletin Blooper</u>
The ladies of the church have cast off clothing of every kind. They can be seen in the church basement Saturday.

My favorite story about stylistic performance comes from a seminar experience where a young, enthusiastic musician was conducting a movement from a Mozart Mass, asking for romantic tone, much *rubato*, and somewhat sentimental phrasing—in other words, lots of conductor, not much composer. When asked *why* he was doing the music in this way, his reply was: "Because I feel it that way." The instructor, in cold, reptilian tones replied: "We don't care how you feel it—how does Mozart feel it"?

How the music "goes" is crucial for those of us working with volunteer, amateur singers rehearsing once a week for Sunday services, including high holy days and the occasional longer work. We encounter a wide variety of musical ability and varying levels of commitment. The attempt is to prepare anthems, hymns, and responses Sunday after Sunday—and there is never enough time!

A Definition of Style
How do we define "style"? I'm glad you asked. Style is the right (appropriate) sound, in-the-room, taking into account the players and singers and asking the following questions:
- What kind of piece are you?
- Do you have brothers or sisters?
- Are you recorded? Are your siblings recorded?
- What is written about the time in which you lived?

Invariably someone asks: "How fast does this piece go?" To which the answer is a question: "Who will sing it?" (Women?

Men? Combined voices?) "Where will it be sung?" (What is the acoustical environment?) "What will it take for this piece to sound and live in a comfortable environment, and be known for what it is and where it comes from?" The choral equivalent is "I know your people."

A Look at the Current Scene: Some Observations

1. Anthems, hymns, and responses sound much the same in tone, articulation, dynamics, and phrasing (if any). Much of the conducting and playing is the same regardless of the piece.

2. Often, we know enough to enable our choirs to sound and sing better (more stylistically) but our various frustrations, mainly that of time, defeat our best intentions and we sink back to the average, the norm, the usual—the dull!

We go to workshops, read periodicals, seek advice, then return to that bass on the back row with arms folded in reaction to the first notion of something new or different. As one of my choir members says loudly enough for all to hear: "He's been 'workshopping' again."

Negative voices can finally defeat even the most industrious, the most enthusiastic, the most positive.

A Look at the Current Scene: Some Suggestions
1. Variety Is the Spice of Choir Life

If one leafs through a denominational hymnal, most hymns look alike. Yet, deeper observation reveals a treasure trove of differing styles that require different ways to sing and play and articulate! I will refer again to Alice Parker's book *Creative Hymn Singing*, for it is a basic text in style, interpretation, and articulation. I commend its study, not just for hymns, but for the differences that delineate style periods. Parker provides concrete suggestions as to performance practice. Using the great variety found in the hymnal is a way to stretch the music budget and bring variety to rehearsal.

2. Use Variety in the Rehearsal Format

Differing anthem styles automatically allow for a change of pace—a valuable commodity in a fast-paced, once-a-week rehearsal. Later discussion will center on a sample rehearsal plan, but just as preaching from the Common Lectionary often forces a look at unfamiliar texts, so choosing from the wide variety of music and hymns available contributes to our own growth and to that lively rehearsal we all want.

3. Use Variety in Your Approach to Ministry

Some who come to your rehearsal have high commitment and demonstrate regular attendance. These "core people" are the lifeblood of the ensemble. They deserve your best expectation of what can be done and a challenge that makes their time spent worthwhile. There are always those who are less committed. Some present problem personalities. Let's face it: choirs attract the unusual (strange?) because with us they can find a home. We all have our share of "interesting" singers and a part of the job is to care for and nurture *all* of the flock, while continuing to push for growth and change.

All in the flock require personal time—that phone call or written note or pat on the back is crucial. We owe to the most committed our best work, our highest expectation, and we shouldn't allow those most on fire to be cooled off or watered down by the less enthusiastic. The tension, however, gentle reader, can be fierce. Someone has to be out front beating the drum, giving the signal, rallying the "troops." Guess who? You!

4. Your Choice of Literature Is Crucial

Here is my checklist for choice:
- What is needed (appropriate) for the service
- What is needed to sustain growth
- What I need to challenge my growth and effectiveness

In my experience, there is always tension between realistic expectations and challenge. Says Paul Oakley:

> It is easy for the successful choral conductor to continue to build a small repertoire of "quick-fix" methods and pieces, and never grow to a higher level. The successful choral musician constantly faces the need to confront the challenges presented in the study of a new score. Each score presents opportunity to learn new techniques and philosophies already in practice. Choirs that sing the same anthems

from year to year become stagnant and bored. The result is a form of brain-death.

A healthy choral program must maintain a balanced repertoire just like a healthy person must have a balanced diet. A choral program trapped in a choral style, or trapped in a period of music history, suffers a musical and cultural malnutrition.[1]

The Tension of Choice

This tension occurs in balancing the practical demands of producing something Sunday after Sunday, with an artistic criteria of producing something well sung, in tune, with appropriate tone and style, and intelligible text.

People sing in a choir to give service to their church and voice to their faith. It is appropriate to work on what I call "choral hygiene," that is, vowels, consonants, breath connection (support), agility, range, dynamics, articulation, mood, color, and nuance, in order to have a good "performance." Remember Deschner's definition of "performance" from chapter 4.

Embracing this philosophy, our rehearsals can be well paced, lively, energetic, begin with solid tonal concepts in the warm-up and continue through a variety of musical styles and difficulty. This is exactly what our people want, and it is cheaper than therapy! They come stressed, pressured, poor (most of them), and pooped! They leave refreshed, enlivened, and energized because that is one of the gifts of music in an ensemble setting. To ask for less than their best is to deprive them of just this experience that they, and we, need so desperately.

In the Beginning Was the Concept

Because we are always rushed, and there never seems to be enough time to accomplish the task, we are tempted to go for the "right notes" at the expense of the spirit and life of the music. We fall into what Alice Parker calls the "reading syndrome": the "let's learn the notes and rhythms and let the conductor supply the interpretation" way of thinking.

It is a misunderstanding to see the page as a basic source of information which, if followed exactly, will yield a usable product.

(Imagine a recipe, followed exactly, with no care for the freshness or flavor of the ingredients.) To "improve" the product, one can't just add a few seasonings—one has to go back to the beginning with new ingredients and a new focus: flavor FIRST, not last.

In music based on text, the "flavor" begins with the text. Not just sacred or secular, or what it "means" but how it feels in the throat (vowels and consonants), and how it flows and captivates on the tongue of a loving reader.[2]

I will discuss rehearsal planning later in chapter 6. For now, remember my personal credo: From the very beginning, every aspect of your work should be a musical experience. Informed score study confirms everything known about the style of a particular hymn or anthem. This is the "how" ("where") I begin with after careful study. I begin with color, nuance, shape, sound, phrasing, articulation. For me this means:

1. Almost never just "reading through" a piece—interesting and challenging for the good readers, but frustrating for many.
2. Almost always beginning with text as described by Parker—speaking and listening to word shapes, meaning, rise and fall, and looking for phrase destinations. Often I introduce an anthem by:
   a) All reading the text aloud, not in the rhythm of the music, but in the rhythm, color, and sound of the text itself.
   b) Reading again, listening for the variety of enunciation, color, and nuance possible, and exaggerating the differences.
   c) Reading again to enjoy the feel of vowels and consonants in the throat.

Here is another rule of thumb:
• Speak for meaning.
• Pause for importance.
• Linger to love.

Though this may seem slow, we gain in the long run. Most of my folks have trouble handling text and tune at the same time. When we approach the music by the "reading syndrome" (get the right notes, put in the phrasing, enunciation, and color later) we most often get a sameness of sound and articulation that I characterize as the "Holy, Holy, Holy" sound—that is, singing everything in four parts, homophonically, fairly square, and flat-footed musically. Is this too much of an indictment of our profession? I think not. It is not meant critically—it should be obvious that I understand what we face. But we can and should sound better—all of us!

In the Beginning Was the Concept: The Text

From the beginning, aim for a musical experience. This is my credo. For me this means beginning with the text, spoken for meaning and nuance. In a delightful article in *Melodious Accord*, Alice Parker makes a case for what she calls the "Backwards Method" of learning:

> In studying scores of music with text, begin with the words, and never lose sight of them. Don't play the notes on the piano or listen to a recording. Sit back in a comfortable chair and read and enjoy the poem, and ponder the musical ideas and forms which develop from it. How would you set this text? When and where did the composer live, and how does this place relate to that world of sound? Learn the time relationships by conducting, always hearing the text inflections. The last thing you do, after outlining the form, and studying all the other markings on the page, is to sing and play the notes, within the style.

> In teaching these works to your choir, use the same sequence. Don't, please, teach them the notes-and-rhythms on the page then add the words later. It simply doesn't work—the words are never able to generate the line and become squashed into the notes. If your choir can speak an entire anthem without pitches: words, rhythm, color, mood, dynamics, accentuation, formal structure, contrast, etc., with wonderful communication of the text, then you are in the best possible position to drop the pitches gently onto the words without losing the spoken values.

> Of course, there's lots more to score study. My guiding principle is to try to recover the sense of immediacy that the first writer or singer must have had. If I were the first singers of this song, who am I? Where? What has happened that makes me have to sing? The context dictates the sound of the song, and the structure of the piece grows out

of that specific sound. When we can balance the large structure and the smallest details of articulation, we make music.[3]

"When we can balance the large structure and the smallest details of articulation, we make music." Indeed!

In the Beginning Was the Concept: The Breath of Life

More important than any one single ingredient in music making, and the one I fail most often to hear in workshops around the country, is phrasing: that is, thoughts that go together toward a destination. I never hear enough air or enough space in the music. As solo singers we were all trained to stand in the crook of the piano and mellifluously intone "mah-may-mee-moh-moo" in the most connected and resonant way possible: "in the mask." In this fashion, many of us developed the vocal instrument. When we use our "vocal instrument" by laying it on whatever piece comes along, we fall victim to the "o-ye-of-the-flesh," instead of the "o-ye-of-the spirit." We have endless variety in articulation, tone, color, and nuance at our disposal, but we often settle for a bor-ing ren-di-tion, not al-low-ing for any rise or fall. When we weight all words the same, we get boredom and singsongy renditions. When we fail to see the destination of the phrase, we fall victim to a boring product.

There is never enough listening to what Parker calls the sound-in-the-room. My teacher, Bev Henson, used to say that "one phrase must let down before the next one picks up." Our attention to note values and the like becomes our God, instead of what actually sounds expressive musically. It need not be so.

This should not be read as license for the kind of mindless interpretation we so often hear in the guise of: "I feel it such and such a way." "I think it should go like this." Our preeminent question should always be, not "How do I feel it?" but "How does Mozart feel it?" I plead for better listening, more enjoyment of smaller units, more awareness of the cumulative effect of several phrases coming together to make a musical whole.

Choirs can be trained to lift without breathing. That mark (a comma) can do more to enhance what I've been talking about than any other single articulation. A lift can break a long phrase into something shorter and more interesting:

Faith while trees are still in blossom, plans the picking of the fruit
Faith can feed the thrill of harvest, when the buds begin to sprout.

In order to make the music lively, interesting, and full of breath (and breadth) we must break things up. Consonants come ahead of the beat consciously (like the double consonants in the words *glory* or *praise*), interior consonants always need to be overdone, and final consonants should be appropriate to the context. Our groups are pretty good on initial consonants (except for those pesky ones that come ahead), miserable to lousy on those "in the interior," and often overdone on final consonants—a sort-of "take that" kind of choral "consonnation." (Not a real word—one I made up.)

Breath anticipation is so vital to the musical product—not only rhythmic breath, but also breath full of the color, life, nuance, and understanding of what is to come. Choirs are often late because breath is lazy. Choirs are often late because we sing all notes full value, thereby slowing the entire process. Dots don't need to be sung, and a tie is as good as a dot. The sign in our room reads: DON'T WAIT—ARTICULATE!

As an example of much that has been discussed above, let me turn to a favorite: "Harvest of Faith." The piece satisfies my criteria of choice: a meaty text with matching, well-set music. Dr. Lovelace has created a bright, bouncy, jazzy tune with a running bass accompaniment that lights up and enlivens the text.

In teaching this anthem, I begin with the text, speaking, not in the rhythm of the music, but in the word rhythms. If I don't immediately get to the rise and fall of the words, I'll get a "notey" rendition because "we" will make all the words the same. Again, I call on Alice Parker:

> If the conductor learns the music principally from the page, with a metronome, characteristic text inflections tend to disappear, and each beat may sound with the same weight of accent. How bor-ing-it-would-be-if-we-con-ver-sed that way—yet this is one of the traits which seems to define "church music" or hymn: the poetry, the expressivity is smothered under a flat-footed equation of quarter note to syllable.[4]

I tell my folks, "You have elevated *of, the, and,* and *to* (to name only several) to world-class status." This accounts for that "boring" style of which Parker speaks. When we weight all the words the same, we give all words importance and lose nuance and inflection. I speak of lightening up certain words, pausing, enjoying the trip, then moving on.

After the text, I would deal with this delightful tune: splendidly crafted, witty, enjoyable in its own way, partaking of an upbeat (anacrusis) impulse throughout. The tune dances and we approach "on our toes," not in galoshes or flat-footed. The best way I've found is to use a Swingle Singers approach, singing on doo-bee-doo-bee-doo, instrumentally, perhaps even moving a bit. Imagine, that St. Swithins-in-the-Swamp choir even moving at all when they sing! To call on Robert Shaw again:

"Anacrusis" is Greek in derivation, and means substantially up plus to strike (our upbeat is about as close as one can come in translation).

For whatever complex of psychological, physiological and neurological reasons, given a repetitive pulse, the human mind appears to desire to group that reiteration into patterns of strong and weak, or heavy and light. (The clock does not say "tick-tick" or "tock-tock.") And it would appear that the normal, more frequent, and more satisfying grouping is light to strong, or upbeat to downbeat, rather than the reverse. (The clock says tick-tock.)[5]

So the approach to this tune is upbeat, even (and especially) the first note. We've been taught that you give a downbeat after a bar line, but I suggest that you begin with a lifted feeling, as if the notes in the first measure were a series of upbeats: light–light–light; light–light–light–strong–light.

Faith   while trees   are still in   blos - som

Ask "them" to sing on doo-bee-doo in this manner. Your demonstration of weight (dancing with upbeats) and your accompanist's helpful, light playing will bring results.

If "pounding" the pitches would really help, all of our choirs would sound better. Sometimes we just need to take a section out and "pound" them. Relax, I'm only kidding. If we were to take seriously modeling with our voice exactly what we desire in the way of shape, nuance, tone, destination, and articulation, then listening to "them," continuing to nurture the product creatively and positively, "they" will get it—they really will!

After separating text and tune, we put the two together and take care not to let a "notey" performance occur. If it does, go back to doo-bee-doo and try whispering the text in rhythm. Make a game out of parts of the text, asking each section to be ready to take up where the other section left off at your signal.

We can develop in ourselves the ability to see music beginning with the large structure down to the smallest detail of articulation. We can fall in love with poetry, meaning, shape, and nuance. We can discover wherein lies the musical life of the piece and, often, it is text first, then music.

Moreover, we can develop in our people their ability to recognize the overall form and shape of the piece, to love the poetry, mastering the vocal ability to use the appropriate sound, sensitive to all of the nuance, shape, flavor, and sheer fun of vocal performance. So often, volunteers can accomplish this because they don't know they can't. Blessings on you. They are worth it.

Notes

1. Paul E. Oakley, "Artistic Choral Singing for Adult Choirs," Masterclass publication.

2. Alice Parker, "The Backwards Method" in *Melodious Accord* 2 (June 1995): 1.

3. Ibid.

4. Ibid.

5. Robert Shaw, *Choral Journal* (January 14, 1986): 7-8.

CHAPTER SIX

If It's 7:15, Where Am I?
Rehearsal Planning

Bulletin Blooper

The Senior Choir invites any member of the congregation who enjoys sinning to join the choir.

OK! They are seated in front of you, holding your choices of music. You are standing in front of them having studied your choices. Now what?

Prologue

Helen Kemp, that wise Mother Superior of children's choir work, has two important rehearsal dictums I always try to remember:

> **PLAN YOUR WORK, WORK YOUR PLAN.**
> **ANALYZE, DON'T RATIONALIZE.**

To "plan your work" means to consider the following rehearsal elements:
1. A variety of choice in anthems, hymns, and responses
2. Attention to what is upcoming and immediate
3. A written plan with assigned timing
4. Careful score study
5. Attention to demands of ministry, group building, and morale

Variety of Choice

Given the demands of your particular situation, your resources, and your worship service and physical setting, variety in anthem choice is one key to a successful rehearsal and ministry. As stated earlier, the choir will not improve without challenging repertoire, but "challenge" should be tempered with realistic appraisal. A balanced musical diet with short-range and long-range goals keeps interest high in weekly rehearsals. The wise director will not try to be "all things to all people" in the St. Paul Choral School tradition, but will strive for balance both in choice and in presentation. To be courageous, smart, caring, and shrewd in planning and carrying out the task is essential.

Rehearsing the choir's role in service music (hymns, responses) and cultivating their understanding of this important task is crucial. This element of worship leadership usually has to be consciously nurtured. We hear: "If we're only singing a hymn, I'm staying home." Truthfully, leading the congregational choir is our *first* priority. When that prayer response or benediction response you rehearsed once over lightly bombs on Sunday, almost everyone knows it. Congregations can smell fear and also sense when something is not "quite right." That puzzled look some choir members give you right *after* the pitch is sounded for a response and right *before* you are to sing, does not inspire confidence in the director. It's the deer-in-the-headlights kind of look, which you know means: "I have no earthly idea what we are doing." It is guaranteed to knot your stomach big time!

After the choir is well rehearsed to lead the congregation, the skillful director will seek to build a trust level with those in the pew, choosing the simpler responses, antiphons, and so on, whose success is well assured, then proceeding to the more challenging. More about congregational song in chapter 9.

Planning and Scheduling

If you schedule carefully, with realistic assessment of the preparation needed, you will prioritize rehearsal time based on this realistic assessment. This *should* mean that anthems are ready when scheduled. Nothing is so awful in a rehearsal as that feeling of pressure generated when not enough groundwork has been laid and the choir simply is not ready. In those cases, it is usually better to substitute rather than to "face the music," if you'll pardon the bad pun. My carefully worked out schedule often has to be readjusted as I go. Our motto is: We will sing no anthem before its time. One learns to estimate the appropriate time required or one suffers along with composer, choir, and congregation.

Score Study

Before discussing a practical process to make the above discussion real, I want to call in three of my teachers, whose perspective on *looking* at music is paramount to score study, which is paramount to a good rehearsal sequence. There is no shortcut. My joking statement to my choirs always is: "I know that I'm not Robert Shaw, but just remember: you're not the Robert Shaw Chorale." In all honesty, most of us would like to be at the end of the journey, knowing what there is to know about a piece of music, but to trudge over all those hills and valleys isn't fun. Here are some ways to take that trip.

Coming to Grips with the Page (Ann Jones)

The following represent notes taken in a seminar given by Dr. Jones. I assume full responsibility for my understanding of the content of her talk.

1. Know what the pitches are. This means playing and singing each line, circling mistakes made when it is sung, and deciding how each line works and how the lines interrelate. "There is pitch—then there is pitch." Note where good intonation might be faulty, circle awkward voice leading and intonation problem places. Rehearse descending scales and think sharp.

2. Know accurate rhythms. "There is rhythm—then there is rhythm." She spoke of vitalizing the subdivision.

3. Know the dynamics. Note the proper dynamics. It is important to rehearse *under* the dynamic.

4. Adjust the balance. Figure out where the composer or arranger has not done his or her work with balance. Shift the number of voices; that is, add voices to adjust balance rather than say "sing a little louder."

5. Pay attention to diction. Note difficult diction problems and notate correct diction in your score.

6. Note the appropriate style. What is on the page doesn't represent practice. (That is performance practice or "how the music goes.") Dr. Jones maintains that breathing places have much to do with stylistic performance. Breath marks are not sufficient. We should ask our groups to mark exact releases (where the "t" goes, for instance).

7. Recognize learning styles. People learn in a variety of ways—

aural, visual, and so on. She suggests devising an exercise to treat a particular intonation or rhythmic problem, then going to that place. When you do this, you are also creating a rehearsal plan.

Structural Analysis

Always start with the overall forms: measures, subsections, bar groupings, scoring (who plays/sings), key, time signature, tempo (learn the music *in a tempo*). Learn to rehearse structurally. "We have a responsibility to let our people know what we know."

In choosing a tempo, find the fastest note value and correlate with what is known about the acoustic environment in which the piece will be sung with the speed of the harmonic rhythm.

Articulation: The Conductor's Responsibility

The conductor's responsibility is to understand phrasing—the relationship of *all* the phrases. We communicate through text articulation and fabulous dynamic.

We should have an informed context or style, and know what conducting gesture will work to bring that style about. We should have insight into the poetry and give thoughtful attention to it.

When we speak of articulation we really speak about duration and how duration affects attack and release. Our job is to communicate effectively. Two things remain: (1) Your superior ear, and (2) your musical imagination.[1]

Tasting the Page (Alice Parker)

This information is excerpted from an editorial in the *Melodious Accord* newsletter, June 1996.

Earlier, Parker spoke of the "reading syndrome," which she characterizes as "let's learn the notes and rhythms and let the conductor supply the interpretation" way of thinking. Parker maintains that "it is a misunderstanding to see the page as a basic source of information which, if followed exactly, will yield a usable product" any more than a recipe followed will yield delicious results without regard to the "freshness or flavor of the ingredients." What follows then are excerpts—all from Parker:

> In music based on text, the "flavor" begins with the text. Not just sacred or secular, or what it "means," but how it feels in the throat

(vowels and consonants), how it flows and captivates on the tongue of a loving reader. Why teach the even quarter notes first, if the students will eventually have to break between the 3rd and 4th for a comma in the text? Why let them sing words on automatic pilot (a series of pronunciation gimmicks) rather than with a poet's understanding of their sound and structure? Why not breathe with the text, rather than with the measure line? Why ask for staggered breathing? We all have to breathe: let's use it positively, for expressivity, rather than negatively, to imitate some instrument not dependent on air.

For me, the durations on the page are as close as I can get to duplicating for the eye what I'm speaking/singing aloud when I read the text well. I am not squeezing the syllables into the noteheads; I am allowing the pitch to clothe the vibrant reading with its own magic. And how about those pitches? Are high notes the same as low, in their production and sound? Should a forte high F in the soprano sound as loud as a forte low D? Not for me: I want to hear a difference. Is there one desirable vocal tone irrespective of register and style, like canned soup? Or are there hundreds of homemade variants.

How about the differences between volume and intensity? Which carries further: sheer loudness, or the will to communicate? And. . . does it matter where we sing? The page can't help us here, moving from live hall to acoustically dead or from indoors to out. How about the size of the group? the style of the music? the formality or informality of the concert?

On most of these questions, the page is little or no help. What CAN it do? It can transmit the baldest information about text, pitches, rhythms and performance values across time and space. Like the recipe, it cannot guarantee edibility. The capacity for discriminating taste marks the good cook—as the discriminating ear marks the musician. The good cook reads the page within a context of experienced sounds and practices techniques for bringing them to life.

Just as a recipe, even in Julia Child's hands, can't solve every cooking problem or guarantee success—so a page of music is only a set of instructions to the singer. Approaching it with love and understanding is the first requirement. Interpreting it with eyes, ears, and mouth open is the second. And the third? Take them both with a large grain of salt: trust your senses! Enjoy! [2]

An Approach to Music: The Purpose of Analysis
(Julius Herford)

Analysis can help us understand the score well enough that we are not swimmers driven by a sea of emotions. Analysis lays bare the skeleton, but the bones should not show through in performance. We will study the technique of composition, that the spirituality of the composer may reveal itself to us.

It is a false tradition to eternalize something without understanding its purpose. Our love of Beethoven must urge us to find his essence of thought.

The multitude of single notes hides the original vision of the composer. Our inner ear conceives this vision. We analyze to try to find the path that leads into the very spirit of that incarnated in the sound.

There must come a moment when one senses the entity of a work, but does not yet know the details of the work. There must be avoided the moment when the details are known but the sense of entity is lost.

As a conductor you are also your own audience. Listen to what happens within. The people sitting there must not keep the music from coming into existence. In your closed eye have the soul of other people. As a conductor you are alone. We are born alone and die alone, and we are alone whenever great things happen. This makes us brothers. Courage is the basis for doing wonderful things in life, to see mistakes and go back once again, coming closer to the truth.

Instead of reading the music for the first time, it is so easy to fall into the habit of turning on the phonograph. This prevents us from contacting music directly without the mediation of an interpreter. Feeling helpless, again and again we must confront the music silently with our mind and ears. We must expose ourselves to this situation, so that we may become readers. A musician is not entitled to listen to a recording until he has an idea of his own. It is shameful to only copy what another conductor does.[3]

The Practical Process (John Yarrington)

At the side of the page, I list all anthems, hymns, responses, descants, for each Sunday—at least six weeks' worth. I double-check the schedule so I don't overlook something. For me, there is always about thirty minutes' of work on a major piece built into a two-hour rehearsal. I know that I work on a cumulative effect because of fluctuation in rehearsal attendance. In other words, I have to be smart about apportioning time and emphasis or I'll get caught trying to accomplish too much in one evening—frustrating for me *and* for "them."

The music needs to be "in the bones." The three R's of rehearsal are REPEAT, REPEAT, REPEAT, with creative repetition. I frankly love to go back to a piece we have performed because we can let more of its beauty and clarity unfold as we grow in our understanding. As a corollary, we should repeat anthems more frequently than we do, I believe. We hear the music week after week in rehearsal, but the congregation only gets one shot. I have often thought about singing the same anthem three Sundays in a row, changing the title ("Psalm 150," "Praise Ye the Lord," "Come Before the Lord with Praise") to see if *anyone* would notice. Also remember that congregational attendance fluctuates as well. They deserve another hearing.

Begin on Time

A successful rehearsal begins on time with careful warm-ups made interesting by variety and approach. The warm-up should lead directly into a hymn or anthem in a good state of readiness, one with high comfort level for the singers who have learned a good sense of style, color, nuance, and so on.

Gradually, movement is toward the major emphasis(es) of the evening—the hardest work—then tapering off with easier, less demanding pieces. I like to have announcements about one hour and fifteen minutes into rehearsal, but keep them brief, then continue to taper, finishing with a short devotional. Often my folks pick up a sheet with pertinent information about the upcoming Sunday, with constant emphasis on major events and dates.

The Routine (Mundane)

When most of the routine items are handled: seating, folders, hymnals, agenda on the board, and so on, more time can be spent on music making. Volunteers are guaranteed to waste time getting their "stuff" if it is not readily available. Good librarians are worth everything—they help keep the troops supplied because some are always clueless (see earlier philosophy on "Is this tonight's music?"). There is a form, an ebb and flow, to a successful rehearsal akin to a well-constructed piece. When our rehearsal is finished, there should be a sense of fulfillment, of accomplishment. Does this always happen? Of course not! Do *we* get frustrated with *them*? The reverse is also true.

Expectation

The more I expect *them* to see and hear what needs to be done, the better the product. If I expect skillful, artistic, colorful texts, full of nuance and meaning, *they* have to accomplish this. My job is to raise awareness of the entire ensemble. If I expect tall vowels, full of beauty; diphthongs with appropriate weight and emphasis; and crisp, effective consonants, I must work on these aspects of our music making diligently, even relentlessly. Someone asked the other day: "How long do you rehearse?" Answer: I (with emphasis) rehearse for two hours! How often at 9:00 P.M., with fifteen minutes to go, I am still at it, while most of the troops have checked out. Their bodies are still in the chairs, but it is brain-dead city!

Bev Henson always told us: "Ask your singers to do what they can do—and be specific." I love the story about the director who kept yelling "BLEND, BLEND, BLEND" to her choir. Finally, one weary member raised a hand with the following statement: "We'd be glad to *blend*, if you'll tell us *where, when,* and with *whom!*"

At Union Seminary, many years ago, a group of us were discussing our rehearsal procedures, particularly as related to singing along with our group. After all the ideas for what was good about "assisting" our singers, one brave soul said: "I sing with my group because when I sing with them *I can't hear them!*" In the next chapter, we'll discuss "Fat-Free Conducting." Suffice it to say, for the present, the more we run around, stamp, clap, tap, and sing with our groups, the less we raise their awareness of their part of the job. And *we* are pooped in the process!

To the notion that it may not be "Christian" to work on the above (subtext: you are on an ego trip) I remind all of us of Roger Deschner's definition of performance: "Performance simply means to complete what one has set out to do, to accomplish it with the special skills that are required."

Robert Shaw once said:

The understandings of the spirit are not easily come by. It takes a creative mind to respond to a creator's mind. It takes a holy spirit to receive the Holy Spirit. And "Just as I Am" is not nearly good enough.

To those whose mentality, if not their actual comment is, "I just gave this (their voice, their solo, their ensemble, etc.) to Jesus"—I think, most sincerely and reverently, Jesus answers: "Take it back"![4]

Guiding Principles

So, if it's 7:15, where are you? You are in a rehearsal with people about whom you care deeply, who will stand up next Sunday and sing "something." People matter! The demands, wants, needs, and concerns of those who make up the choir are crucial to the project. Your care and concern expressed in cards, calls, hospital visits, and so on, are ministry in itself. Equally important is your role as the choral leader, one who sets the pace. Care in matters of choral hygiene (beautiful vowels, crisp consonants) elements of phrasing, blend, musical sensitivity and intelligibility means that you care for them chorally, as well as personally. Balancing the demands of ministry is both joy and pain! Expectation should be high. People will respond to it. Your love shows in your care for their personal welfare as well as this choral well-being. We should never excuse poor performance in the name of ministry. God loves a well-tuned chord and well-prepared choirs. We praise with our whole being, and worthy praise, well sung or played, helps us remain whole.

So, you are there and *they* are there. I pray that *they* and you (and I) will be ready.

Notes

1. Dr. Ann Howard Jones, from unpublished class notes.
2. Alice Parker, "Tasting the Page," in *Melodious Accord* 6 (June 1996): 3-4.
3. Dr. Julius Herford, from unpublished class notes.
4. Robert Shaw, lecture given at the University of Oklahoma, November 19, 1977.

CHAPTER SEVEN

Conduct Yourselves Accordingly
A Fat-Free Conducting Diet

A bean supper will be held on Tuesday evening in the church hall. Music will follow.

Recognizing the difficulty of talking about something as indefinable and personal as conducting, without being able to demonstrate or to observe, might be the equivalent of "take two downbeats and call me in the morning." Here is an attempt, however, to put into perspective some observations and suggestions about what music makers do as gesture to bring about a musical product—not what one *says*, but what one *does*.

Conducting Credo
I believe in a standard "grammar" of conducting, which includes:

- How and when to start (qualities of beginning)
- How and when to stop (qualities of ending)
- How loud, how soft (range of dynamics)
- How fast, how slow (range of tempi)
- Degrees and varieties of articulation (prosody, text beauty)
- Beauty, direction of phrasing ("beginning, middling, ending")

I believe that singers and instrumentalists should be trained to respond to standard gestures that are universally known and understood, to bring musical results.

I believe that singers and instrumentalists must be encouraged to become part of the musical product—to make *ensemble* a real word.

The Current Scene
In a paraphrase of Ross Perot, "This is what I've learned, watching people all over the country conduct."

1. There is too much physical involvement: sweating, swaying, grunting, singing, clapping, tapping, yelling, bouncing, bending.

2. Many get over into the performer's area instead of receiving the sound, attempting to make people play or sing, rather than encouraging, influencing, bringing about with them a total musical product. When we reach toward them, we invade their space, we look awkward, and our conducting efficiency goes down.

3. Conductors *move* instead of *use* the frame. Our body serves as backdrop to our conducting. When we sway, bounce, move sideways, and bend, we make that backdrop ineffective, dissipating energy, reducing conducting effectiveness, in short: wearing ourselves out.

4. The tendency is to talk rather than demonstrate.

5. Singers/instrumentalists are not trained to follow and respond to simple gestures ("grammar") even though many have participated in successful high school or college choral programs. They usually are inexperienced in responding to this basic grammar because many conductors, who often are supremely musical and knowledgeable, talk and teach their way through the music, using a special set of personal gestures known only to the initiated. The product is often marvelous, but at what price?

When these singers come to you, in your church choir, they truly don't know, in many cases, how to respond, even if you are very clear. Sometimes you have a special set of signals, which they now learn and the cycle continues. How much easier it would be for all of us to deal in a standard currency?

6. When we step in front of an instrumental ensemble, using this special set of signals, we are in trouble. What's more, many instrumentalists think badly of "choral" people for just this reason. It need not be so.

Point/Counterpoint

I can hear someone saying: "I have to clap, tap, stamp, sing, in order to get some energy and life in the sound." We all know what that means. The ratio of conductor effort to choir performance on the volunteer level is probably 80 percent (conductor) to 20 percent (choir) if we are lucky. All of us who exhort children, youth, and adults in a church situation relate to this "cheerleader mentality."

I also hear someone saying: "You are asking me to stand still, use more economical gestures, slim down (slim-fast) my gestures, and I feel that I am not involved in the music enough. This makes me feel emotionless." The following is my answer.

Fat-Free Conducting Checklist

Teaching conducting really requires personal interaction, much like teaching voice. Someone must make gestures, someone else must evaluate them and make suggestions. If you were to come to me, the following would be my expectations for you:

1. Learn to economize (less is more). Conducting efficiency is the goal.
2. Learn to receive the sound—not reaching, bending, swaying, but learning to make contact with the sound you hear.
3. Separate your hands for maximum efficiency.
4. Use your stance (backdrop) to your advantage.
5. Enable them—learn not to cross the line between conductor and singer or player.
6. Experience the power of "elongation."
7. LOOK like the music SOUNDS.
8. Develop fluency with a baton.
9. Learn to balance perspiration with inspiration.
10. Practice "dry conducting."
11. Have the score in your head, and your head out of the score.
12. Develop precision and poise—the sense of someone in charge.
13. Work on musicality.

I would want your personality to shine through in your conducting, but always in the service of the music. All excess gesture should be eliminated. Your strength is in clear, precise gestures that convey not just the technical demands of attack, release, and dynamics, but also the spirit and life of the music. This is not most effectively conveyed by your swaying and sweating, nor can you, as the conductor, sing or play the music yourself.

Prescription for Success

1. Identify three fulcrums: wrist, half arm, whole arm. Practice using only wrist, only half arm, only whole arm. Think of it as a Jane Fonda workout. Isolate those fulcrums and begin to look for places in the music you conduct where you might use only wrist, only half arm, and only whole arm. Probably, we use a lot of half and whole arm and not much wrist. Practice patterns in 2/4, 3/4, and 4/4, using the three fulcrums. Stand tall. Watch yourself in a mirror for signs of reverting to the "old practice."

2. Separate your hands: with your non-baton hand, using a cupped gesture, practice using only that hand in a simple rising and falling motion. Add basic patterns with the other hand. This is a bit like rubbing your stomach and patting your head. Be careful that you don't reach out toward those you plan to conduct.

When you acquire some facility, begin to practice giving cues on specific beats or cutoffs on specific beats. When we conduct using both hands and arms all the time, we have no way to cue, outline dynamic or articulation variety, or show the shape and destination of phrasing.

Where did we get the idea that conducting is somehow "natural" and that no practice is required?

3. Get a baton. Not one with a light on the end, and one that is not too short. Generally, the tip laid against midpalm with the handle at the elbow joint is a good length. The stick should point forward—it is an extension of your arm. Practice simple patterns. Being careful not to wobble (don't conduct with vibrato), give a clear downbeat about waist-high, with a good ictus or bounce, followed by clear ups and downs or sideways gestures. Stay within your frame or backdrop. Don't hunch over, bounce, sway, bob, grunt, and so on. Remember: Less is more.

4. Study the anthems you are going to conduct so that, in your newfound conducting freedom, you will know *what* to conduct. I encourage all of us to hone our investigative score study skills to enable us to be creative in the ways we teach. Asking the right questions of a piece enables us to know what makes it tick, anticipate problems, and to be "smart" in the introduction and subsequent rehearsals. The better we know the music, the more we can encourage a great degree of musicality by our conducting, not

by our talking. Enable your groups by careful score preparation, lively, creative teaching, and clear conducting gestures.

Coda

There really should not be the perceived dichotomy between "choral" conducting and "instrumental" conducting, but as long as many of our number subscribe to a special set of conducting signals, physical gestures known only to the choir initiates, we will, in my opinion, be much less successful and expend a great deal more effort than is needed. Additionally, we are perpetuating the special-signals conducting approach to our detriment.

Here's the scoop: what is not efficient needs to be eliminated. Useless motion, twitching, swaying, hunching of shoulders, leaning over, gestures too large—any excess, no matter how learned or practiced, can be excised. New techniques feel uncomfortable at first. I encourage you to practice on "them." Don't give in to more cheerleading than you absolutely have to. Work on making your "grammar" clear, and expect your choirs to speak that same language.

The spark that ignites the great performances often comes from the inner spirit of the conductor as he or she guides and infuses a performance, at once accurate and musical. Your investment in group responsibility for being part of the music making, the way in which your teaching and pacing in rehearsal have caused the singers to have a firm grasp of the various elements of the piece, and your willingness to expect "them" to respond to simple, basic, standard conducting gestures, make exciting performances possible. We should do no less.

Perspectives on Conducting

The second half of this chapter deals with observations of several conductors whom I consider role models for what music makers are about. I take full responsibility for my observations, recollections, and quotes. The intent is to informally share impressions and understandings gained from these master teachers.

Don Neuen

In a week-long session with masters students at Southern Methodist University, Dr. Neuen was, from the first, energetic and articulate—he has one of the highest energy levels I have observed.

The warm-ups incorporated both the essence of style and articulation and the sound desired for, in this case, J. S. Bach. The sound became buoyant, ongoing, with a lift, with no talk *about* music.

From the first, the form and shape of the piece were revealed. What was primary material (trumps) was revealed. This is only possible because of detailed and exhaustive score study and an understanding of the history of the particular performance practice.

The expectation was to sit up, *act* like singers, *look* like singers, *sound* like singers. The entire approach was exceedingly vocal, evidencing both a great love for and a good understanding of the voice.

Much was overdone both in singing and in conducting in the rehearsal. In the performance, the conducting was invitatory; Neuen was always there in preparation. He didn't say "Look up" and then look down at his score! He physically turned, moved, and invited the players to join. Great energy was expended by him in look and gesture but the conducting was refined and elegant and, from the back, never called attention to itself. Why? Because Dr. Neuen had done his homework with the score and worked on the most important aspects of the piece contextually. Result: A lively, energy-filled presentation of the evening's music. Said Dr. Neuen to the chorus: "You have never looked more alive."

Some assorted quotes:

- "Don't be careful—work for energy—find the energy."
- "Nothing is as boring as accuracy."
- "You must ask yourself as a singer: 'Would anyone want to hear what I am doing?' "
- "You may not perform in an ordinary manner."
- "Don't be conservative in using language (foreign)—it *sounds* like it is not right."
- "Proclaim! Present! Perform!"
- "The key to all music is forward motion—by emphasizing offbeats, we get forward motion in harmony and rhythm."
- "There should never be two notes back to back with equal emphasis."
- "You won't succeed without concepts—vowels, original material, and so on."

- "Singing is no different from the communication of the greatest actor."
- "No one gets a good choir—it has to be built."
- "Text is the most important thing—it is our life!"
- "Never assume that you know enough about tempo, and dynamics and style—work with a musicologist. A conductor always needs a teacher. He (or she) is only as good as what he knows."
- "Our lack of knowledge inhibits the potential and success of people capable of succeeding." (Wish I'd said that!)[1]

Ann Jones

She defines conducting as a series of preparations—every beat sets up the next one with gestures unaffected by mannerisms of any kind. (Preach it!)

When you walk into a rehearsal with instruments it is helpful if you don't have to change technique.

When you pulse the subdivision, it makes the singers late.

Look like dancers—not flailers.

My favorite Ann Jones quote (at the end of a rehearsal): "Your clothes are sopping wet, you are exhausted, and your people say: 'What was that all about?' "

Some other memorable quotes:

- On score preparation: "Do you practice what you are going to show?"
- "We have responsibility to deliver the meter."
- "Don't get in there and make noises with them."
- "Engage the music maker in the rehearsal."
- "Think of 'etching' the shorter notes."
- Definition of music: "The persistent focus of one's intelligence, aspiration, and good will—not a luxury but a necessity."
- "Singers want demands made of them."
- Another favorite term (for singing posture): "Body attitude."
- On tone: "A radical commitment to the vowel. We have to know what we want to hear—what color—everything else is easy." [2]

Bev Henson

Technique is everything—being able to analyze rapidly (chorally) then demonstrate in facile conducting. Knowing is not enough! Change in the music should show in the conducting—the inexperienced conductor tends to look for only big changes.

Time is the canvas for music. Change is the only true constant of time and of music. Change happens when the words change. The idea is to define technique, like fingering for the keyboard. A stick (conducting baton) is essential.

Notation tells us *where* a note starts, but not how long; most important, which notes are long and which are short.

There is always primary material available. The primary material will always become secondary to the new primary material.

Clean up your act! Get rid of extraneous gestures that do not speak.

Stance/Balance: Stand on both feet and don't move your feet. People don't see your feet, but they do see when the feet move.

The boring part of your job is what you are paid for—anyone would want to do the "good" choir.[3]

Rodney Eichenberger

I found most interesting an article in the *Choral Journal* (May 1996) by Alan C. McClung with a title only a mother or a dissertation committee could love: "The Relationship Between Nonverbal Communication and Conducting: An Interview with Rodney Eichenberger."

> We do not hear with our ears only; we do not see with our eyes only; both these senses go together and form a whole which makes human communication complete.[4]

McClung, a Ph.D. candidate in choral music education at Florida State University, provides an overview of literature on nonverbal communication, as well as its effects on conducting, and concludes with an interview with Rodney Eichenberger, a leading expert on nonverbal communication and conducting.

In the article, Allen T. Dittman points out:

> People communicate through words, tone of voice, facial expressions, body movements, proxemic behavior, and by psychophysiological responses such as blushing and speed or depth of breathing. Nonverbal communication comprises such a significant portion of human interaction that health professionals have determined that it even plays a role in mental health.[5]

Having observed Rod Eichenberger on several different occasions, and copied some of his nonverbal gestures (which really work), I was interested in what he had to say about this area of nonverbal communication:

> Virtually all conductors I know have developed conducting habits that are sometimes antithetic to the desired effect. Those habits are usually reactions to some kind of frustration. As a result they start pawing for the music; their motions get bigger, and their control is decreased. They start telling them what they want over and over again; however, they are unconsciously showing the choir something contradictory. Conductors should coordinate intent with verbalizations and gestures in order to give consistent messages to the choir.

> I think that we don't teach conducting adequately if we don't carefully investigate all the possibilities that nonverbal language brings to the communication between conductor and performer.[6]

Eichenberger, in response to questions posed by the reviewer, is asked to focus on three or four primary areas that relate to the development of nonverbal conducting skills.

1. Posture

Posture includes the placement of the feet, the movement of the knees, the movement of the head, and body balance. When the conductor's knees are moving, one of the first things I do is stop the conductor. I demonstrate what happens with just a single note while bending the knees: the pitch sags. That nonverbal message implies sitting down, which in turn results in a downward direction in pitch.

Similarly, if the foot, elbows, head, or wrists are keeping time, the primary rhythm is disturbed. It creates an extra focus point for the singers' eyes. The performer must decide which to follow, the foot, the elbow, the head, the wrist, or the hand.

2. Visual Aspects

I am convinced that the more one is drawn into the visual aspects of another person's movement, the more one will imitate that action. I remember my first experience with a

Cinerama movie that had a scene involving a roller coaster ride. As the roller coaster went around a corner, the entire audience, sitting in absolutely stationary chairs, went around the corner in their chairs. They moved backward and forward, then up and down. I was intrigued with the degree of empathy that the audience had simply because of the visual stimuli around them.

When I work with a choir that has a bad intonation problem, I watch carefully what the conductor is doing. I can usually relate the out-of-tune singing directly to the conductor's gestures.

My premise is that nothing is right and nothing is wrong, but everything you do has an effect.

3. Standard Conducting Patterns

The incredible importance of being able to conduct steady beats shouldn't be questioned. The beat must arrive at and depart from a single defining point. Rounded beats with circles or smudges give performers options to decide where the beat is.

Music making is determined not just at the point of the beat but throughout the pulse of the note prior to that beat. What happens between the beats determines whether I want to listen or not. The tension-free motion of arriving at and departing from the beat gives music that specific quality.

I encourage your careful reading of this article.

CONDUCT YOURSELVES ACCORDINGLY
Course Expectations and Explanations
(Given to beginning conducting students on the first day of class)

Dear Friends:

On an evaluation from last semester, someone wrote: "Dr. Yarrington's teaching style is not like any of the other Perkins faculty." Another student remarked in response: "That means, it isn't dull." I know how to conduct and I can teach you if you will listen and be willing to try some different approaches, techniques, and so on. I don't want you to look like me; I want your personality to shine through, but always in the service of the music. I will expect you to eliminate all the excesses of gesture to which you are accustomed. When you cross that line between conductor and chorus and orchestra, you jeopardize the result. You must learn that less is more. You can control the sound, speed and shape of the music. You enable the music making by receiving and molding the sound, always with gestures that unmistakably convey what, in your judgment, the composer wants.

When you conduct for a grade, you will be rated on the categories you see on the attached sheet; with each category having a possible score of 10, thus making 100 a perfect grade. So much of this work is subjective that it is really difficult to give something an 8 or a 6 or a 10. Nonetheless, so that there is some basis for grades, we will use this form. Let me elaborate briefly on each of the categories.

Score Mastery

Nothing gives you security and power like knowledge of the score you plan to conduct. Here at school, you will often be dealing with larger and more difficult pieces on the whole, but in the real world of church music, you must produce an anthem(s) weekly with amateur singers. This means at least two things: first, anthem literature will sometimes be easier than major works, and second, you may, therefore, be tempted not to do the same careful score study as if you had Brahms's *A German Requiem* to conduct. I encourage you to be "faithful in all things" and to hone your investigative score study skills. Ask the right questions of a piece, figure out what makes it tick, anticipate problems, be creative in ways that enable your group to sound better because you know the score. If the anthem is easy, commit it to memory and conduct "sans score" on Sunday.

Posture

Your carriage in front of the group encourages their participation in the composer's intentions represented by you. Learn to stand tall, do not wiggle, sway, lean, stomp, grunt, and so on. Work within your frame, using it as the backdrop for your gestures to the group. Receive the sound, be in contact with it, but do not try to lean over and make someone play or sing. You really cannot do that anyway and you just wear yourself out. Ann Jones says: "The rehearsal is over and you are sweating profusely—your people wonder, what was that all about?" There is a line we conductors should not cross. We should maintain our poise and posture to command the respect and attention of the group. Our job is to train them, encourage them, enlighten them, inspire them, but not to get in their way. Your conducting gestures, at once economical and effective, convey the sense and spirit of the music to the group. Any unnecessary movement of frame or gesture weakens the musical result.

Stick Technique

Most of you will be in jobs that expect anthems or major works with voices and instruments. From brass quartet or string quartet to full orchestra, the usual practice is for the conductor to use a baton. You will be better served if you have a technique employing the same, which you may or may not use, than never to have had the experience. Many "choral" conductors do not subscribe to a standard grammar of conducting, choosing rather, a series of physical gestures known only to the choir initiates. These special, secret signs baffle the orchestral member who expects to look up and see downbeats, clear cutoffs, basic patterns, and the like. Anything else results in, at best, a terrible waste of time and, at worst, chaos! Therefore, my friends, you will use a baton most of the time in class.

Use of the Left Hand

"We are a Si-a-meese, if you please" is a cute song that unfortunately often describes choral conductors who duplicate conducting gestures with the non-stick hand. For most, that would be the left hand. You will be given some very simple exercises to free this hand and you will be amazed at the power this brings. Save the "other" hand for specifics of articulation, shape, dynamics, and cueing for greater freedom and economy.

Cueing

Once a score is properly taught and marked by both singers and instrumentalists, your job is to enable the most musical, spirit-filled performance possible, attempting to represent the composer in his or her best light. Singers need precise indication as to attacks and releases and reminders of subtleties of phrasing, articulation, and word shapes. You cannot, however, make them do anything by sheer physical force. When you do, you get in the way of the music's unfolding and look foolish in the process. As for the competent instrumentalists, they usually do not need a dramatic conducting gesture from you. Often, an acknowledgment by looking in their direction will suffice. After sitting for 104 measures without playing, it is comforting to that person when a conductor gives a discreet cue with a gesture or look to say: "Come in now, and welcome to the performance." If the proceedings run amok, if the group speeds up, slows down, plays too loudly, too softly, too *legato*, too *staccato*, your job is to regain control quickly and efficiently. At that point, you are the boss, the "maestro," and you are in charge.

Efficiency of Conducting Gesture

By now you are beginning to get the drift of this paper: what is not efficient needs to be eliminated. Useless motion, twitching, swaying, hunching of shoulders, leaning over, gestures too large—any excess, no matter how learned or practiced, needs to be excised. New techniques feel uncomfortable at first—expect it! Also expect suggestions that run counter to what a previous teacher has said. Welcome the chance to try a new way. Then, you may decide with practice and experience which conducting gestures and signals you will choose to make your own. Remember Yarrington's law: What do they need? More is wasteful!

Precision and Poise

A step beyond elevated posture that gives the conductor a sense of health and well-being and conveys strength, not tension, is that feeling of being in charge. This is an unmistakable signal to singers and players. Another word is *presence*. Even when nervous—especially when nervous—"assuming the pose" will help.

Style

Do we take a conducting style and apply it to every piece conducted, whether or not it fits? Some choruses simply sing with the same tone, dynamic, color, articulation, or lack thereof, regardless of the style. Some conductors simply conduct with the same gestures for all music. Does our study of stylistic differences based on historical reference make a difference in our conducting? Do our ears cause us, in fact, to look quite different in a Gregorian Kyrie than a classical Credo? Asking questions of the particular piece is crucial. Listening to recordings, attending concerts, auditing rehearsals, are all ways to help you decide about appropriate tone, phrasing, articulation, tempo, balance, performing forces, and performance practice. Reading about music is only one frame of reference, albeit an important one. Learning from performance is also valuable. Do not wait until you direct the Chicago Symphony Chorus to begin this quest—start now!

Musicality

In the conducting, is a real musical sense conveyed? Perhaps the most intangible of all the categories for grading is this one. Does all our study and technique result in a performance that is musically convincing and rings true? "Dull" is a four-letter word that should be forever eliminated from the musical vocabulary. No choir has to sound dull and lifeless. The spark that ignites the great performances often comes from the inner spirit of the conductor as he or she guides and infuses a performance, at once accurate and musical. Your willingness to experiment with sound, color, articulation, tempo, and dynamics makes an exciting performance possible.

Overall Impression

All the categories taken together make up this final item in the grading sheet. The word *overall* is the key.

Notes

1. Dr. Donald Neuen, from unpublished class notes.
2. Dr. Ann Howard Jones, from unpublished class notes.
3. Dr. Bev R. Henson, from unpublished class notes.
4. Alan C. McClung, "The Relationship Between Nonverbal Communication and Conducting: An Interview with Rodney Eichenberger," in *Choral Journal* 36 (May 1996): 17-24.
5. Ibid.
6. Ibid.

CHAPTER EIGHT

The Violins Are on Your Left
Working with Instrumentalists

Instrumental Riddles *(in score order)*

Q. How do you get two piccolos to play a perfect unison?
A. *Shoot one.*

Q. What's the difference between an oboe and an onion?
A. *Nobody cries when you chop up an oboe.*

Q. What's the difference between a lawnmower and a soprano sax?
A. *Vibrato.*

Q. How do you make a trombone sound like a French horn?
A. *Put your hand in the bell and miss a lot of notes.*

Q. What's the range of a tuba?
A. *Twenty yards, if you've got a good arm.*

Q. What do you call someone who hangs around musicians?
A. *A drummer.*

Q. How do you make a violin sound like a viola?
A. *Sit in the back and don't play.*

Q. How do you get a guitar player to play softer?
A. *Give him a sheet of music.*

(Anonymous—and for good reason)

Introduction

My friend, Anton Armstrong, has urged me to do for the world of church musicians working with instrumentalists, what he feels I did in my chapter on changing voices in a previous book: demythologize and help, cut through the rhetoric, make this work practical and effective. So, Anton, here goes.

Most of us, in our church life, work at some time with solo instrumentalists, smaller ensembles (brass quartet, string quartet), or a full complement of instruments: winds, brass, strings, and percussion. Usually one of two things happens: (1) we ask (or hire) brass players from the local high school (the award-winning Fighting Eagles Band) to play with us on the morning anthem, expecting accurate notes and rhythms and suitable tuning. Dear reader, it may not be so. Remember that these players work every day, carefully tune (you know, with one of those machines) and go over and over their material. Have you ever heard a high school band tune? What can happen is that they don't have time to adequately learn the material for you and you spend your time in rehearsal just trying to make the music "passable" for Sunday. Or, (2) you hire "professional" players who should be able to play what has been scheduled but you have had little experience and don't understand the instrumental "mentality." The truth is, most of them understand and play their instrument much better than you do. If you study the score, mark parts, have a conference with the concertmaster (if strings are involved), conduct cleanly, ask specifically for what you want (shorter, longer, louder, softer, *poco legato, poco staccato*) and if you understand what singers must do to sing with an instrument ensemble, you have a chance for a good "performance."

This chapter, then, gentle reader, is to help you in your journey through "Instrumental Land," avoiding the pitfalls, understanding the terrain, and making your world a safe place.

Understanding the Instrumental Mentality

Yours truly was up in front of an orchestral ensemble and singers in a workshop with Otto Werner Mueller, Margaret Hillis, and the late Julius Herford. To say that it was a pressure-filled three weeks is an understatement. Our tendency, particularly if we have dealt in choral currency, is to try to make "them" play. Often, we gesture, they play; we gesture, they play; we wait for the sound, they wait for the gesture; and guess what? The music grinds to a halt. Or, we overgesture, in the choral manner, swaying, grunting, huffing, and puffing, which they think is silly and not productive. I was doing the latter, I am chagrined to admit, when Dr. Mueller stopped me with this query: "Herr Yarrington, do you have hair on your baton?" ("No, maestro.") "Can you *play* the violins?" ("No, maestro.") "Let *them* play."

Immediately purchase *Face to Face with an Orchestra* by Don Moses, Robert Demaree, Jr., and Allen Ohmes. This will help you understand the "nature of the orchestra," which is crucial to your musical well-being:

> Choral conductors generally have only limited experience rehearsing and performing with orchestras. Accustomed to the nature and the special techniques of choral work, we may find it strange to deal instead with the expectations and needs of instrumentalists. As a result, many of us prepare ourselves badly for rehearsals and concerts. Working with amateur players, we may not be able to help them enough; working in turn with professionals, we may feel intimidated. In either case, we find ourselves unable to achieve our best intentions.
>
> The problem is not with the players. Most of it can be eliminated by preparation, precise language, and experience. To confront an orchestra with confidence, one first must understand as much as possible about the instruments, the musicians, and their standard ways of communicating with each other.[1]

The authors put into perspective the differences between the training of orchestral players and choral musicians:

1. Orchestras generally have fewer hours of rehearsals and must cover more music more quickly.

2. Orchestral musicians are likely to have had more years of training and experience than the singers with whom they play, or the conductor.

3. They do not memorize the music—thus, they depend very heavily on the baton.

(Parenthetically: If, in the first thirty seconds of the rehearsal, they look up to see you "circling" without a clear downbeat, and attempting to adopt what I call the "Maestro Mentality" without the training or the temperament, they will not look up again. They may play well for you, they will take your money, and then they will speak badly of you [and "us"]. It need not be so.)

4. When players are paid, they are not generally responsive to a "pep talk," or too much talk at all!

5. String players, like singers, work in sections. However, wind and percussion players are soloists—in other words, what they play is "exposed."

6. No pianist is available, as in chorus rehearsal, to help players through difficult spots—the conductor and the ensemble must work these out as they go.

What does this mean to those of us who do not regularly work with instrumentalists, but who want to learn how?

As a choral conductor rehearsing an orchestra, you must expect to cover the music more quickly (stopping fewer times than in a choral session), depend more on the players then you usually do on your singers, refine your conducting gestures and signals (remembering that these instrumentalists are less familiar with you and your intentions than are your singers) and work in a very direct, objective way.

Review your conducting technique. This may be a fine opportunity for you to practice and enlarge your craft. You need not be afraid that any adjustments you make will prove detrimental to your work as a choral conductor; many of the distinctions between so-called "choral" and "instrumental" conducting are more habitual and artificial than substantial.

Neither need you fear that orchestra players will be somehow prejudiced against you because you are a choral conductor by training. It is unlikely they will wonder much about your background, or care very much how you were taught. They will be concerned only with working quickly and effectively in rehearsals to solve their own uncertainties and learn how their own parts fit into the whole fabric of the music. If you are well prepared to rehearse them, and if you treat them in a professional manner, they will respond positively to you and your ideas.[2]

The first half of this wonderful book deals practically with fundamental matters, including discussion of orchestral instruments, ranges, bowing, and so on. The second half deals with three Baroque masterworks: Handel's *Messiah*, Bach's *Magnificat*, and Vivaldi's *Gloria*.

There is no substitute for our own experience, but these authors have simplified the process considerably.

The "P" Words

Philosophy

Chapter 7 speaks of an attitude in conducting where "less is more." We have the idea that if we just exert more, sweat more, grunt more, sway more, clap, sing, run around more, we'll accomplish something. This cheerleader mentality infects our profession. Often, at choral conventions, I shut my eyes because the conductorial act on stage has little or no reference to the music being performed. In her insightful book, *In Search of Musical Excellence*, Sally Herman speaks a philosophy I embrace wholeheartedly:

> One of the most difficult tasks we have as choral directors is to teach our students to sing expressively. Whether we communicate with the conducting gesture, demonstrate with our own voice or another instrument, or articulate what we want, the student must understand what we are communicating. If we teach them to depend solely on us for that communication, we have not taught them to think for themselves. We need to also give them an understanding of basic concepts so that they can become intelligent musicians in their own right.

> Often because of rigorous performance obligations, we tend to spoon-feed our singers just for the sake of getting ready on time. We are placing ourselves in a "Catch-22" because if we do not take time to educate, we will always have the pressure of time breathing down our neck. If our students have a good foundation from which to make their own musical assessments, our conducting gestures are far more effective, we have to articulate less, and we no longer have the need for constant demonstration. After all, our job is to educate and teach our students in a manner that they can make their own musical decisions. It would be a crime to make them dependent on us for those decisions. As was previously stated, the best favor we can do for our students is to teach them in a manner that allows them to have no need for us.[3]

Practicality

I encourage practicing the craft of conducting. Where did we get the idea that we can simply stand up and effectively gesture without rehearsing the physical motions? Like dancing, diving, swimming, golfing, playing football, and so on, conducting is a skill level endeavor that can and should be practiced.

Try, for instance, using only wrist, half arm, and whole arm as suggested earlier in low, middle, and high levels. Practice separating hands: work on the weak hand in simple ways to make it both more expressive and more useful.

In mixed meter pieces where many seem to crash and burn, work out the patterns and practice them so they become natural and effective. Practice on your choir, expecting them to actually produce music from your gestures. Don't cross that line between conductor and performer, receive the sound, encourage them to sing and play (you can't make them sing or play anyway) and train them to respond to your clear indications.

When you work with ensembles, make a map and establish your physical surroundings. I have even placed stands and chairs in the exact configuration I plan to use so I can get used to looking at the appropriate spot. Nothing is more injurious to one's credibility as a dramatic gesture to the left for a timpani entrance, only to have the sound of the timpani come from the right!

I always make a diagram of seating with the players' names. "John, could we have a bit more on the oboe line." These folks have names and have worked long and hard to perfect their craft. Often they are treated as "the oboe player" or "the flute player" as if they had no personality. You will be amazed how the sound of one's name causes a player to sit up and play better.

Purpose

Cleanliness really is next to godliness. It frees us to make music; it frees us to listen to what really is being produced, not what we hope is sounding or what we hear in our head. If we discipline our music making by fat-free gestures, practicing a standard "grammar" of conducting, we become better stewards of our precious time, better listeners, and better music makers. Let them play!

The "F" Words

Frame

In conducting, our body becomes a frame or backdrop for the gesture. When we move, sway, bounce, and so forth, we weaken this frame or backdrop and thereby weaken our gesture. This does not mean we become rigid, but our presence, shown by an alert, tall body does indeed "frame" what we do. Conducting students, especially those who "feel the music," always hate to be told to stand still but this cleansing treatment is just what most need. Our body language conveys much more than we know and when we reach over, hunch down, spring up, gesticulate wildly (especially if things are not going well) we again weaken the product, not to mention beat ourselves up for no good purpose.

Focus

There is an intangible quality of "presence" or "focus" readily apparent in a successful conductor, singer, or speaker. We say that someone "takes the stage" and we know what that means. You convey to your singers or players the sense that someone really is in charge. Your strength comes from knowledge of the score and practice of the craft of conducting. Anything else is false pretense. Most of the successful music makers I know possess this quality, which is not to be confused with the "Maestro Mentality." As one of my teachers used to say: "Remember, 'temperament' is 99 percent temper." Positive reinforcement of our musical goals is the best medicine:

> I can state today that the artistic results of my work with singers, choirs, and orchestras in the opera house and on the concert platform must be ascribed . . . to educational endeavors. I think my musicians and singers will acknowledge that, far from being put under any pressure or compulsion, they were encouraged to obey their own inner urge in their playing and singing, and that my constant inspiriting served to stimulate them to give of their best in the common effort, and to participate in my intentions.[4]

Frivolity

Richard Allin wrote a piece entitled "Conducting Car Concert," which I always try to share at workshops. Here is an excerpt:

> Radio generally has something for everybody—easy listening, rock 'n' roll, rap, country and western, big band classics—and sometimes you can tell to what a neighboring car is tuned just by looking at the driver.

Cars can be nice places to entertain oneself. I conduct the major symphony orchestras when I'm behind the wheel. Indeed, many performers sit behind steering wheels. A few days ago Beethoven's *Egmont* Overture was pouring from the speakers, and I was helping it along with conducting gestures, indicating louds and softs as needed, and generally controlling the tempo.

I was leading the Berlin Philharmonic at the time and was pleased that the musicians could follow me so well. I speak virtually no German. As I molded one phrase palm up for a diminuendo, I glanced over at the fellow driving the car in the next lane. It was clear that he was tuned to the same program and was also directing the Berliners.

He seemed to be a disciple of Leonard Bernstein, making boldly dramatic gestures with the invisible baton. I have been through the Bernstein period and am now conducting after the form of Fritz Reiner . . . I find economical gestures better suited when driving a car in heavy traffic.[5]

The "S" Words

Score

Knowing the score: Nothing substitutes for this knowledge and nothing gives one more security on the podium.

Marking the score: There are standard markings that instrumentalists understand and that you can learn. Get some help from a string player and save yourself some time and trouble. If necessary, sing to this person the articulation you want and let him or her show you how it might be marked. Instrumentalists grumble about too much marking sometimes, but if they receive a score with no markings, they make some immediate assumptions about you and you surrender to them much of the articulation. It need not be so.

Saving (Yourself)

As mentioned, your swaying, sweating, and grunting get in the way of the music. We think we are accomplishing great things, but our perspiration should have been used in score study, not in the conducting.

Working with Amateurs

I mentioned asking brass from the award-winning Pioneer High School Band to accompany a Sunday anthem. Here are some things to remember:

1. They are used to repetition and much rehearsal. Don't assume anything—tuning, correct pitches, accurate rhythms!

2. Work with them ahead of time. Go to the school—take the time. You'll wish you had later.

3. In general, until they "get it," let them play louder than you intend. One of our problems with brass and choir, for instance, is always balance. In the beginning rehearsal with brass alone, however, let them gain their confidence by "blowing" a bit more. When they accompany the choir you can achieve balance quickly by asking them to play shorter (in general) and blow into their stands.

The choir can never outsing a brass ensemble, but they can out-consonant them, out-attack them, and so forth. The good coming to a choral ensemble who regularly sing with instrumentalists is inestimable. It saves them from the choral mentality where someone always saves their bacon by allowing them to be sloppy in entrance or exit in the name of choral beauty and tone.

4. Insist that everyone play on the ictus, the downbeat. Don't let anyone get away with late entrances, brass or choir. Encourage everyone to "participate in your intentions." The clearer, cleaner, less ostentatious your gesture is, the better chance you have for a splendid performance. (Remember, *performance* is not a bad word.)

Anthem with Solo Instruments

Any C instrument sounds where it is notated. Flute, oboe, or recorder can be read and played directly from the score. Often, especially with flute, taking the part up an octave helps its sound.

Transposing instruments are another matter. An obvious example is the trumpet. You will be in for a shock and a terrible experience if you don't know that when your choir sings "Holy, Holy, Holy" in D major, the trumpet part is written in E major, a whole step higher. It sounds in D major (what a relief!) but is written in a key one step higher. The clarinet is also a transposing instrument. *Face to Face with an Orchestra* takes you through this clearly. If you write a descant, for instance, for trumpet, clarinet, and so forth, it must be written a whole step higher than the hymn it accompanies. One also has to be concerned about ease of range, especially with amateur players. Don't be afraid to ask or to consult a text to get an idea about appropriate range.

The Brass Quartet

Typically, many anthems are written for choir and brass quartet (two trumpets, two trombones.) These four can also be used to accompany the hymns of the morning, either in a specific written arrangement, or writing soprano and alto parts for the two trumpets (a step higher) and asking the trombones to play tenor and bass directly from the hymnal. Trumpets or trombones can play the solo hymn line to add color. It is wise not to use all instruments all the time. Give them (and the congregation) some relief. Remember, their "chops" are not those of a professional player.

Again, rehearse them separately (two rehearsals are better than one) and get them into the acoustical environment ahead of the choir rehearsal. Tuning from the organ, for instance, is quite different from tuning that machine in the band room, or even a piano. If organ is to be used, they must tune to it, and changes in room temperature can mean quite a difference even from one service to the next. When instruments and organ pipes are cold, pitch will certainly be different from when both they and the room are warmer.

In the rehearsal remember to ask for what you want in clear terms: shorter, longer, louder, softer, more separated, more *legato*. Think about articulation in these terms. In general, with brass, shorter is almost always better. One stout trombone can wipe out a willing but weaker church choir on most Sundays.

The Rehearsal

With amateur or professional musicians, the following have proved to be helpful to remember:

1. Play and sing through without many stops. Giving instructions before or during only impedes the progress. Face the music, hear what "they" are doing, then decide how to "fix" it.

2. Choirs are notoriously lethargic in a first encounter. Encourage them to "get with the program" ("get on the stick"), anticipating their entrances especially. Rhythmic breathing the beat before is one way to get precise ensemble.

3. A lot of sound is coming your way: don't panic! Let them play and sing, and you listen. Get out of the way with your conducting so that you *can* listen. Sometimes we are literally scared out of our "battle plan" because so much "noise" is coming our way. Our job is to sort it all out, and to be specific in what we ask for. "All right, let's do that again" is not guaranteed to bring much success. Do *what* again?

4. Don't be afraid to ask for what you want but don't act as if you know more than you do. Deal in the common currency of shorter-longer-louder-softer, as mentioned above. Remind the choir of the importance of rhythmic breath and consonant articulation. They cannot outsing a brass quartet or a larger ensemble, but they can out-consonant them. Consonants are our bow strokes.

5. Often we are trained to sing *into* notes. When we sing with instruments, we do better to shorten notes—especially at the ends of phrases before the next phrase picks up. When we sing into a dotted note, for instance, the next attack will almost certainly be late. So, we "slim-fast" that note, getting off, so we can retake the next attack. Choirs are often lazy, and we let them get away with it! If we encourage (insist) that they *mark* as well and learn the discipline of this kind of ensemble, "they" are always better.

Remember: pencils are a sign of intelligence. "I'll remember" is not useful. I always say: "Mark your music so it can guide you in the performance." My friend, Dr. Jan Harrington, at Indiana University, always said: "I want to see flashes of yellow (pencils) in front of my face." So might it always be!

Notes

1. Don Moses, Robert Demaree, Jr., and Allen Ohmes, *Face to Face with an Orchestra* (Princeton, N.J.: Prestige Publications, 1987), pp. 3-4.

2. Ibid.

3. Sally Herman, *In Search of Musical Excellence* (Dayton, Ohio: Roger Dean Publishing Co., 1996), p. 50.

4. Bruno Walter, *The Conductor's Art*, ed. Carl Bamberger (New York: McGraw-Hill, 1965).

5. Richard Allin, "Conducting Car Concert," in Our Town, *Arkansas Democrat-Gazette* (November 1989).

CHAPTER NINE

A Person of Several Voices
Congregational Song

Bulletin Blooper
Sin for Joy.

A delightful article by Scott Corbett in the *Atlantic Monthly* (1955), is the reason for the title. He says:

> For a long time I thought my singing voice was unique. After all, there are 642 hymns in our church hymnal and not one of them is written in my key. This is all the more remarkable when you consider that I have three distinct and different voices to draw on. I have a sort of automatic transmission built into my throat that would probably be of considerable interest to the eye, ear, nose and throat crowd.
>
> My two special voices are my falsetto tenor and my equally falsetto bass, or *basso non tutto profondo*. Then my true voice is a fringe baritone, which is obviously not what the average composer of sacred music had in mind when he penned his vocal arrangements. As a general rule, I try to get around this difficulty by singing harmony, but my improvised harmonics are given to an occasional clinker, and all too frequently, a succession of wrong guesses leads me into a dreadful cul-de-sad-sac! Then there is nothing to do but clutch at the melody line with whichever of my falsettos seems closest, an undignified procedure at best.
>
> One Sunday, after the closing hymn, a particularly intricate Welsh dirge had left me wandering distractedly in the lower octaves, I burst out of our village church in a cantankerous mood. I thought mine was an unusual case—until I mentioned my predicament to some of my fellow worshippers.
>
> Since then I have made quite a study of church singing, and it turns out that I have plenty of company. I find there are two classes of church singers: warblers and mumblers. The warblers think they can sing; the mumblers can't and know it. This is a subtle distinction, but important. The warblers usually wind up in the choir, and the

mumblers make up the congregation. Oh, there are also the mutes, but you can't class them as singers. They merely hold their hymnbooks open to see if the rest of us are singing the words right, and to see how much longer it will be until the hymn is over. The more conscientious among them follow the words with one finger, and occasionally you will see one whose lips move, but that is only because he always moves his lips when he reads. I haven't much use for mutes, I might as well admit it—I feel that mutes are people who just don't have enough guts to be mumblers. In our church we have about a dozen warblers and forty to fifty mumblers, but the dozen warblers make ten times the noise we do. If we mumblers had to sing alone, without the choir, you wouldn't be able to hear us as far as the vestibule. In fact, the only way you'd know we were inside would be from the coughs. We can sing softer and cough louder than anybody.

When I found out how common my problem was, I thought I saw some exciting possibilities. Where can I get in touch with a good live-wire hymnbook publisher, I wondered. All they'd have to do is to put out a hymnbook with all the hymns transposed into our key. Wouldn't work, said another mumbler promptly. Choir couldn't sing 'em then. Besides, said a second, what is our key? I'll bet we all have different ones. Maybe so, but we must all be in the middle somewhere, a lady mumbler pointed out, because, if you'll notice, the hymns are all either too high, or too low.

Well, I wish I knew more about music, because I feel certain that if anybody can solve these technical problems and come up with a good mumbler's hymnbook, he'll have the cleanest best seller since *Little Women*.[1]

What I Believe About Warblers, Mumblers and Mutes
(A Philosophy for Congregational Song)

In his book, *Christian Hymns Observed*, Erik Routley observes: "What is needed for the improvement of hymnody just now is not exhaustive knowledge, but an insight into what happens when people sing them."[2] I respond to the word *insight* because, if we truly are interested in enhancing, encouraging, enlivening congregational song, "insight" into who sings, why, when, where, is crucial. Often, I fear, what I term the "Marie Antoinette" method of hymn singing is adopted, which could be characterized as "let 'them' sing—or not—I know what's best for them."

I've adopted some rules-of-thumb over the years, not seeking to be all things to all people, not adopting a wishy-washy stance, blowing with every wind (new or old) but believing in and trusting the people who sing—it's *their* song, after all:

1. Who are the hymns for? (An answer to that gets one a long way down the road to *what* is chosen and *how* it is presented.)

2. What best serves the needs of a particular day, moment, emphasis? As the one who chooses, I have obligation to minister to many needs and to be conscious that sometimes, the "feeling level" of the service is best enhanced by the right hymn. It doesn't have to be great music or text to be appropriate to serve the need. (Heresy?)

3. The hymns are not *mine*, but *ours*.

4. Organists need be reminded that they have an endless supply of wind (or electricity), but singers have to breathe!

5. "Raising" standards (a common plea) usually results in only "raising" hackles. Taste in music is very personal and associative or historical (sometimes hysterical). We deal with emotions and taste as pastorally as possible but without the pejorative stance so often adopted: "I know what is best for you."

6. Not all hymns need to be sung. Look for ways to use texts spoken corporately, or set up in litany fashion. Most people react to, respond to, and love the *tune*, not the text. It was Routley who said that "hymn singing is an unthinking habit." We sing things we have no intention of doing: "Take my silver and my gold, not a mite would I withhold." So, to raise consciousness of the *text* is a worthy goal.

A digression. A book no longer published, *How to Become a Bishop Without Being Religious*, has served as fodder for many a talk by yours truly. Written by Dr. Charles Merrill Smith, this satire "stabs people awake" says Bishop James A. Pike. That it does. Listen to advice given in the chapter on "Conducting Public Worship":

It will strike you as you pore over your hymnal, that the preferred subjective-type numbers in most cases have texts which are little short of gibberish. What does it mean, for example, when that grand old favorite of the years, "Sweet Hour of Prayer" has us sing,

Till, from Mt. Pisgah's lofty height,
I view my home, and take my flight:

93

Somebody's Got My Robe

> This robe of flesh I'll drop, and rise
> to seize the everlasting prize,
> and shout while passing through the air,
> Farewell, farewell, sweet hour of prayer?

If you didn't know this is part of a hymn which has comforted countless Christian souls, you might take it for a message in a code which defies all efforts to break it. Nor can you escape the conclusion, as you segregate the good hymns from the bad ones that very few modern, prosperous, comfortable and contented Christians can sing these precious old religious ballads and mean a word of what they are saying.

Picture if you will, the successful, hard-nosed executives arriving at the church in their Cadillacs and Lincolns, dressed in Society Brand suits with their wives in mink stoles joining in,

> Others may choose this vain world if they will,
> I will follow Jesus;
> All else forsaking, will cleave to him still,
> I will follow him.

Or imagine the president of the local bank chanting,

> Take my silver and my gold,
> not a mite would I withhold.

Or a wealthy bachelor with a stable of comely lady friends and a taste for exotic foods and rare wines solemnly intoning,

> Earthly pleasures vainly call me. . .
> Nothing worldly shall enthrall me. . .

Or the average collection of Christian saints who know full well that the church is split into denominational segments too numerous to count, pooling their enthusiastic voices in,

> We are not divided, all one body, we,
> One in hope and doctrine, one in charity.

Here is a mystery. How can relatively sane, intelligent people happily sing what amounts to nonsense, or claim, through song, to believe what they obviously do not believe, or promise via hymnody to do what they haven't the faintest inclination to do, and would be stunned if, after the amen, were told to go and do what they just finished saying they were going to do: "Take my silver. . ."

The explanation of the phenomenon is obvious. It is that people hardly ever pay attention to the words when they sing hymns. It is as if they know, in advance, that the words don't mean anything anyway. If they like the tune, if it is associated with pleasant experiences, if the music

94

falls agreeably on their ears, they make no demands on the text of rationality or poetic quality or anything else.[3]

A harsh indictment? I think not. I have a friend who says, "When you see 'refrain' in a hymn, you should!" Most people will put up with many verses in order to get to that refrain, whose lilt and rhythm almost always is tune-oriented. I once led a hymn sing of refrains only with great success. Forget those time-consuming verses—on to the refrain!

What is important is an attitude on the part of the presenter, the leader, who recognizes that the above is pretty close to the truth and that our stance for success is to invite and encourage participation firmly but lovingly—one might say pastorally.

7. Build a "trust level" with your people by an inviting, hospitable approach.

8. Stay away from too much talk. If information about Ralph Vaughan Williams would cause people to sit up in their pews and sing better, I'd advocate it. Truthfully, I believe they couldn't care less. It is those of us "trained" in classical music who want to impart our knowledge and "lift them up." Our study of Ralph Vaughan Williams should enable us to teach and encourage our people in a more creative fashion. They won't even know what hit them.

Creative Hymn Singing

It should be obvious by now that Alice Parker has had profound influence on my music making. What she says about singing, after a lifetime of involvement with a cycle of choosing a text, setting it to music, hearing it rehearsed and recorded, then revising it for publication, has given her what I believe is the best insight to congregational song in our country. She proves time and time again that she can *do* what she *says*. She is able to take an "average" congregation, as well as a room full of choral directors, and get them singing—and loving the process and the product. Truly, hers is a gift of song.

Her book, *Creative Hymn Singing*, is a result of her hands-on approach and an unwavering belief that people want to sing melody and countermelody, unaccompanied, often at their own speed, without being "led" by an organist, who is more interested in preludes and postludes than in enabling congregational song. If hymn accompaniment, loudly played on the organ, would enhance congregational song, many more congregations would sing better. Throw out the organ? I think not. You will read what John Ferguson thinks about this a bit later on. I never want to be characterized as "anti-organ" but rather, as "pro-congregation."

Often, our tendency is to sing hymns in a "church style," without much thought to the profound differences found under the cover of most current hymnals:

> We take the hymnal for granted. Because each page looks alike, we tend to think that the music should sound similar. A quick glance at the dates and geographic origins of the hymns demonstrates that there can be no such thing as one common hymn style. These tunes and texts are as diverse as the societies that produced them, and with a little imaginative effort, we can begin to recreate their original function and sound and thereby make the music live again.[4]

The basic organization of this collection is historical with most of the discussion directed to the tune:

> One of the glories of music is that it says what words cannot say; and one of my aims is to help reestablish our respect for the music over the words of the hymn. The music should always be performed in its proper style, not modified to fit a certain text.[5]

The intent of the collection is to provide "musical ideas for the improvisation of hymn-anthems by choirs and congregations." Parker believes that an "old-fashioned song leader" is essential for this process:

> When the leader has asked and answered enough questions about a melody to be able to place it in time and space and function and sound, he or she can begin to project appropriate settings for it. Not harmonizations: pianos and organs are built for harmonies. Voices want to sing melodies: counterpoint is the natural extension of sung melody.[6]

With a Little Help from My Friends

From *Christian Hymns Observed*, by Erik Routley:

> Hymns are delightful and dangerous things. They are regarded, in the late twentieth century, as inseparable from the worship of all but a very few Christian groups. They are as familiar an activity as reading a

newspaper: in worship they are for many people the most intelligible and agreeable of all the activities they are invited to join in or witness; they are the most easily memorized of all Christian statements, and one who has not been in a church for most of a lifetime, but who was brought up in church when young, remembers some hymns, though everything else may be forgotten.

Hymns are a kind of song: but they differ from a professional song, or an art-song, in being songs for unmusical people to sing together. They are a kind of poetry, but they are such poetry as unliterary people experience; and if the poetry is too weighty for the music to get it moving, it won't move; while if the music is so eloquent as to drown the sound of the words, the words, no matter what nonsense they may talk, will go clear past the critical faculty into the affections.[7]

From an article in *Circuit Rider* (October 1995) by my friend Dr. John Thornburg, entitled: "Beyond Hymn Selection":

Meet some of the demons we must exorcise if we are to unleash music's power:

The pastor who doesn't even pick up the hymn book during congregational singing. Being a musical non-participant is not neutral; it is counterproductive. Let go of the myth that the sermon is the only real event of grace and embrace the reality that the Holy Spirit uses every moment of our worship services. We are so certain that only the spoken word can save that we don't allow music to play its own role in salvation.

The pastor who covers his or her lack of knowledge by being rigid. Knowing the music of the church is a critical part of pastoral care simply because music is so often a means of grace. There will be times when a parishioner requests music we don't like, don't know, or find silly. Here we need equal measures of grace and discernment.

People are often moved deeply by music not because of the poetry of the words or the beauty of the melody, but rather because of where they learned the music, from whom they learned it, and the sense of spiritual presence or community they experienced. As pastors, we must pay attention to this deep reality. We must also remain open to the possibility that God can build community and foster justice even through hymns we may find overly personalistic.

The pastor who says, "I know this music is brand new to most of you and that probably nobody knows it." Talk about a self-fulfilling prophecy! Anyone who introduces music this way deserves the non-response that is bound to follow. I have heard pastors say, "My people only know 25 hymns in the hymn book and those are the ones we're going to sing." If your people only know 25 verses of scripture are those the only ones you're going to read or use as basis for a sermon? We clearly see the opportunity to teach the Bible and we enjoy the moments when a light comes on for someone because we opened up a verse or story for them in a new way. We rarely see the opportunity to introduce people to the richness of the hymnal and other musical resources.[8]

From two articles in *The American Organist,* my friend John Ferguson discourses on using the organ to accompany hymns. It has been my joy to work with John and I know of no other church musician/organist who so ably and creatively puts the "mighty organ" to use in the service of worship. In the December 1994 issue, Dr. Ferguson observes:

There has been a confusion of understanding between the terms sacred music and church music. Sacred music is any work with a religious text or theme. Church music is any work conceived for use in corporate worship. Church music is music which supports, encourages, and does not get in the way of congregational song. The organist functions as church musician when engaging with and inspiring the congregation in its song. Prelude and postlude are nice but unimportant frills in comparison to the primary obligation of organ and organist to sing with and lead the people's song.

In this sense, then, the congregation needs professionally trained musical leadership in order that it may fulfill its liturgical responsibility to be the corporate choir, gathered at worship to sing the story of God's creating and redeeming acts. It is not necessary for a congregation to have a professional musician to provide religious (read sacred) musical entertainment. Rather, the professional is present to help the people find their voice, to encourage and lead them in their song.

The organ remains the single best instrument for one person to use in energizing congregational song. In quantity of sound, in quality of sound, in variety of sound, it is unsurpassed. The organ provides a good bass line, which is the primary way people feel rhythm.

Unfortunately, it seems that the creative possibilities for leading congregational song inherent in the organ and this central dimension of the organ's rule in most congregations are de-emphasized in our profession. Such an attitude is fine if one thinks only of performance. If one thinks about church music and the organist as a church musician, the focus on leadership of congregational song must become more valued and affirmed in our profession than has been the case.[9]

In the January 1995 issue, Ferguson states:

The leadership of congregational song is the reason most congregations engage organists and the primary justification for their investment in a good organ. For most worshipers the organist serves primarily as their song leader, not the provider of preludes and postludes. In many situations, the people arrive after the prelude has begun and are long gone before the postlude is over.

It is easy to become cynical and somewhat bitter over a lack of interest in the instrument we love. Some of our frustration could be reduced if we considered the organ (and by extension ourselves) as a servant to the worshiping life of the congregation. In this context it is important to remember that there is a difference between servanthood and servitude. We are not in bondage to the whims of our congregations; rather, as we understand the concept of servanthood, we become freed to a more enjoyable and satisfying musical life as church organists.[10]

From an article in *Melodious Accord* (1994), Alice Parker writes about the renewal of congregational singing with the title: "How Can We Sing Without the Organ?" Says Parker:

Hymn singing with keyboard accompaniment is so taken for granted in our society that the suggestion that another path might be better is received with astonishment. Yet consider how this practice developed.

We are born with ears and voices, in response to the fact that sound exists. These provide one of the five primary means that we have to learn about our world, and to share that learning with others. We are born knowing how to listen and how to sing.

So how did we get so fixated on organs? Voices came first, with singing of the sacred texts at the center of worship, and all kinds of instruments adding color. Gradually, music making has become the work of professionals, and the individual has been released from the responsibility of contributing sound to the service.

So what have we lost? Modern technology puts great resources at our fingertips, and the organ is a wonderful instrument. It lends all kinds of sonic possibilities to our services, and can indeed, in the right hands, well support congregational singing. But if there is no group sound to begin with, no pattern of participation, no enjoyment in the listening to and contributing to the song, then the organ cannot supply it. It simply cannot teach people how to sing—the sound is produced in a totally different fashion, and there are no words!

One human being who acts as a model for each individual member of the group is the most practical solution: one who knows how to encourage, affirm, line out, guide and listen. This is the historical method for building a singing congregation.

A group that sings well together learns to listen, and opens its collective soul to be moved by words and emotions which touch the innermost being. Protective walls come down as voices join in a sound which none can make alone, which affirms the individual, the group and the tradition.

We need to identify, encourage, and train people in this kind of song leading, and make a place for them during the worship service. This is far from concert conducting: rather, it is drawing sound out of everyday folks: children, babies, older people, those who have been told they can't sing. The whole point is that everyone joins in, and that they make a sound, their sound, *our* sound.

I've never met a group that couldn't sing. But I have found that I must take away the helps: no accompaniment, soloists, or choirs. Let the ministers and choir physically join the congregation, and allow people to focus on meaningful sound rather than on reading music. Once a congregational voice has been established, and people are used to singing at the heart of the service, the organ and choir may certainly enhance the musical experience. But they can never be an adequate replacement for the song of the people.[11]

It seems to me that the popularity of everything from the praise chorus genre to much on the contemporary scene is its accessibility and almost assured success for the singer. Repetitive words and catchy, short melodies with limited range, all invite participation. We can draw our collective liturgical skirts around us, ascend Mount Snobus, and continue to "lead" (dominate) our congregations, secure in the knowledge that we know best what they should sing.

Or, gentle reader, we can roll up our sleeves, believe in them, trust in them, and get on with our task of enhancing, enlivening, embracing congregational song, finding as many ways as possible to build their confidence.

The trust level I spoke of earlier is absolutely essential. In *The United Methodist Hymnal*, for instance, we have a wonderful Psalter with singable refrains. We have wonderful congregational response for Communion and Baptism. If we sing (model) what we want, without explanation, if the choir has been carefully rehearsed and takes its role seriously, if the attitude is one of inviting and encouraging, then after you sing, you hold up your hands in the historical rabbinical tradition and they sing with you and the choir.

Look for hymn segments that everyone sings as Call to Worship, Call to Prayer, or Benediction response. Songs specifically designed as call/response, such as "This Is the Day" (UMH, 657) with words from Psalm 118 adapted by the tune writer, Les Garrett, enliven the beginning of the service and may be sung simply as leader/people. Using an older, familiar hymn as a Call to Prayer ("Sweet Hour of Prayer," "Spirit of the Living God," and so on) creates an atmosphere for prayer when everyone sings. A sung response after the benediction ("God Be with You Till We Meet Again"—Vaughan Williams tune, or the refrain to "On Eagle's Wings") gives a corporate send-off to the service. I also believe that we need to use whatever we are doing for several weeks. As Brian Wren said in a recent workshop, "There is power in the repetition of the familiar." We are often too concerned about changing responses every week—we'd be better off to let the congregation experience them until they become familiar.

Another obvious way to encourage congregational participation is the use of a hymn-anthem in which, at some point, all join in singing a familiar hymn or new words set to a familiar tune. Many of these settings use brass or handbells as accompaniment, in addition to the organ, and the excitement of that instrumental addition encourages everyone to participate.

Alice Parker spoke of getting the choir out among the congregation and I have found this to be very successful, after the choir was convinced they were actually going to leave their loft and join the people by literally surrounding them. An even simpler way is to do a stopped processional or recessional in which choir members stop in the aisle(s), turn in to the congregation for a verse, then resume "coming" or "going."

I look for two hymns that might form a "medley." Here are some models to get you thinking about this possibility:

Palm/Passion Sunday Medley

Combine "Mantos y Palmas" (UMH, 279) with "Ah, Holy Jesus" (UMH, 289) for Palm Sunday. "Mantos y Palmas" is in C major with its distinctive South American flavor, while "Ah, Holy Jesus" is in F minor, somber and serious. What better way to combine the strains of Palm/Passion Sunday? Try this:

- Sing verse 1 of "Mantos y Palmas" (ending in C).
- Begin verse 2 of "Ah, Holy Jesus" in F minor with no introduction (ending in F minor).
- Begin verse 2 of "Mantos y Palmas" followed by verse 4 of "Ah, Holy Jesus."
- Finish with refrain only of "Mantos y Palmas."

Patriotic Medley

- "This Is My Song," verse 1 solo, verse 2, congregation
- "God the Omnipotent," verse 1 solo, verse 2, congregation
- Interlude: "O God of Earth and Altar"
- "God the Omnipotent," verse 3 (interlude)
- "God the Omnipotent," verse 4 (interlude) both congregational
- "O Beautiful for Spacious Skies," verse 1 solo, verse 2 men, verse 3 women, verse 4 all

Medley on Waves and Faith

- "Eternal Father, Strong to Save" (solo, choir on "loo" SATB, verse 2, all)

- "Jesus, Savior, Pilot Me" (verse 1 choir SA, verse 2 all women, verse 3 all)
- "My Lord Came Walking Over the Sea" (verses alternated between choir and soloist, everyone on refrain every time)

A Pilgrim Mosaic
- "I Want a Principle Within" (verse 1)
- "A Charge to Keep I Have" (verses 1 and 2)
- "I Want a Principle Within" (verse 3)
- "Lord, I Want to Be a Christian" (verses 1 and 3)
- "I Want a Principle Within" (verse 4)
- "Ye Servants of God" (all verses)

Many times, we overlook possibilities for *speaking* a hymn, such as "Woman in the Night," the marvelous Brian Wren text with music by Charles Webb. There are eight verses. Have four different women read each of the first four verses, with everyone reading the refrain. Choir women read verse 5, choir men read verse 6, everyone reads verses 7 and 8. If there is a text that is just so appropriate to the service that we want to use it, we can always speak it in various ways. We can, of course, look for an alternate tune, but speaking really opens up understanding.

I have a conviction that when the congregation opens the hymnal and sees a long hymn (more than four verses) or one that spills over to the facing page, they instantly are weary—and wary! Congregational singing shouldn't be an endurance contest. All the more reason for variety in stanzas by changing the accompaniment, designating different segments for verses, using the choir alone, everyone singing one verse *a cappella*, and so on. The more we build in variety the better will be the hymn singing and the corporate worship.

Brian Wren speaks of "butt knowledge," which he defines as the view from the congregation of one who sees it from that side, and often from the same pew. Everything from sight lines to hearing to perception is important to the worship leaders and we should take this "butt knowledge" most seriously. Wren also makes the case for innovation in worship, citing many biblical examples of God doing something "new": the story of the Exodus, the deliverance from Babylon, the many healing stories, and the Resurrection. Wren says it is "traditional" to innovate. We should not be afraid to try something different with our folks, but we should never startle or abruptly change just for the sake of change.

When we build in a trust level, an inviting posture, a flexible worship order—when we have faith in them, we can all enliven congregational singing. We don't need to throw out the organ, but we do need to sing without accompaniment on a regular basis. Wren says that "the familiar mediates the sacred" and we shouldn't be afraid to sing some of the "good old hymns" when appropriate. Sometimes flow, feeling level, a sense of serendipity, can take over liturgical/theological considerations and one is frequently surprised that the Holy Spirit can actually work through some of "those songs." We lead in love. We grow in knowledge. We look for every opportunity to lead singing and to talk to Sunday school classes, board meetings, and so on. We are the musical leaders of our flock and they look to us. What they should see is the best model of a servant-musician, committed to excellence, skilled in knowledge, and pastoral in intent.

Notes

1. Scott Corbett, *The Atlantic Monthly* (1955): 58-63.

2. Erik Routley, *Christian Hymns Observed: When in Our Music God Is Glorified* (Princeton, N.J.: Prestige Publications, 1982), p. vi.

3. Charles Merrill Smith, *How To Become a Bishop Without Being Religious*, (New York: Doubleday & Co., 1965), pp. 84, 86.

4. Alice Parker, *Creative Hymn Singing* (Chapel Hill, N.C.: Hinshaw Music, Inc, 1985), Foreword.

5. Ibid.

6. Ibid.

7. Routley, *Christian Hymns Observed*, p. 1.

8. John Thornburg, "Beyond Hymn Selection" in *Circuit Rider* (October 1995): 6.

9. John Ferguson, *The American Organist* (December 1994): 32-34.

10. John Ferguson, *The American Organist* (January 1995): 82.

11. Alice Parker, "How Can We Sing Without the Organ?" in *Melodious Accord* (1994).

CHAPTER TEN

A Letter to Benji
Philosophical Coda

(Benji is an actual student whom I met at a workshop in North Carolina. He was intent during the sessions and came up afterward to ask about the use [practice] of church music today. This letter is my way of saying what I really believe about the "practice" and the tension involved in serving the church through music.)

Dear Benji,

So good to meet you. You raised some interesting questions about the practice of church music, which I'll try to answer. I am having the book, *Music Through the Eyes of Faith* by Harold Best sent to you from the publishers. Best affirms so much of what I believe about being a "servant musician" and does it convincingly and lovingly. Enjoy!

My thoughts (answers being, perhaps, too strong a word) about your questions come out of thirty years of being in church music in three different churches, where I fought the "good fight" for a ministry that attempted to balance the needs and desires of diverse congregations in a program of music involving singers and ringers from ages 4 to 104. *(A slight exaggeration.)* Mostly, it worked, though there are scars from both the "purists" and the "regulars." I've served two annual conferences in planning worship events, rubbing shoulders with clergypersons. I like being with the clergy! Frankly, I often prefer their company to that of some musicians I encounter. Through their eyes, my church world was redeemed over and over again.

There is, I believe, constant tension resulting from discussion of what is "appropriate" or "inappropriate" for music in church; what is "high church" or "low church." And that freighted word: *standards*. I have always espoused the idea of balance in all things, while stressing adequate preparation and performance, whether preaching, reading scripture, directing the choir, playing the organ, dancing, or designing visual aids. There are always those who insist that if you "love Jesus" and are in ministry, whatever comes out of your mouth or your 8' stop is good enough—it isn't! Further, we have, for too long, justified poor preaching, playing, and singing in the name of the Almighty.

I stress preparation as a necessary component of ministry and temper lofty ideals with a good dose of realism. As my former boss and friend, Bishop Ben Oliphint used to say to staff: "You have to work both sides of the street." Of course, Ben also used to say about being employed on a church staff: "It beats working for a living." The tension, Benji, is in the effort to strike a good balance between what is known and what is done. To be in ministry, to choose worship elements with care and integrity, requires energy—tremendous energy! love—tremendous love! and patience—tremendous patience!

Your questions framed themselves around this tension I've just outlined above. When trained musicians encounter a theology that seems to advocate a kind of instantly accessible music, not too classical or "high church," performed by willing, but not too polished singers, directed by a sincere, but not too demanding conductor, often they flee to the hills—or to Amway! If it sounds "too good," in other words, if people are expected to stretch instead of soak, then they "won't come to Jesus."

The church growth movement has focused heavily on the use of music. It is just such use you ask about. In his book, *Dancing with Dinosaurs*, William Easum makes the following statement:

> The type of music that reaches people comes out of their culture. Culturally relevant music can be discovered by determining what radio stations most of your worship guests (not members) listen to. Every survey will show that "soft rock" is the music of the majority of unchurched people in America. Only four percent of the records sold in the United States are classical.[1]

John Bisagno, pastor of First Baptist Church in Houston, Texas, minces no words when he describes the debilitating effects that classical music has on worship in most settings:

Long-haired music, funeral-dirge anthems, and stiff-collared song leaders will kill the church faster than anything in the world. Let's set the record straight for a minute. There are no great vibrant, soul-winning churches reaching great numbers of people, baptizing hundreds of converts, reaching masses that have stiff music, seven-fold amens, and a steady diet of classical anthems. None. That's not a few. That's none, none, none.[2]

Here are some other Easum tidbits:
- "Worship is not the place to teach music appreciation."
- "Synthesizer, drums, flute, electric guitar, tambourine, bass, and piano are the basic instruments of today."
- "Hymnals are often discarded or supplemented with praise choruses that reflect contemporary tastes in music."
- "Choirs are becoming optional and are often replaced by ensemble leadership groups."
- "Changing the music habits of declining or stagnant congregations is proving to be a major cause of conflict. The source of the conflict comes primarily from trained musicians who often find these concepts repugnant and resist any change in the style of music. Church musicians do more to hinder congregations from sharing new life than any other staff members."

This comes from the lens of church growth. What Easum demonstrates is a grasp of what motivates non-church people to join—I have no quarrel with that. My quarrel is with the absolute lack of balance espoused and the indictment of those in my profession trained to do their jobs. Are the preachers similarly to disavow their training and study to proclaim a message of popular culture? [3]

Paul Westermeyer, writing in *The American Organist* has this to say:

Discussions about what music to use in worship often contain an implicit assumption that if you just use the right popular sounds, people will flock to your services. Apart from the demographics of particular places and the naiveté of this assumption, the underlying problem here has been unmasked by Samuel Adler, who comes from a cantorial family and teaches composition at the Eastman School of Music. He says, "The music of worship has been cast in the role of convenient scapegoat for all maladies afflicting the attendance at, participation in, and comprehension of worship services."[4]

Continues Dr. Westermeyer:

This puts the musician in a terrible bind. He or she is perceived as the one who is to market a product whose truth is not the issue. The issue is solely how well the advertising is done and how many customers you can sell on the product. That has never been the role of the church or synagogue musician. It may work to sell carpets or soap or cars, but it's an impossible contradiction for the church or synagogue musician who by it is set against the people as their manipulator, rather than as one who lives with and for them as the leader of their song.[5]

So, Benji, the questions you ask now have some context. Let me attempt to shed some light–not heat.

Those of us involved in choosing music for worship services, weddings, and funerals are often confronted with the difficult task of telling someone that what he or she wants is not, in our best judgment, the most appropriate choice for the event. Your questions, therefore, are most appropriate and timely:

1. Are there articulated rules for measuring what music is "appropriate"? Are "formal" and "informal" helpful terms?

2. Has the church, in liturgy and music, become too cerebral? Are we a people who need help expressing our emotions? Is it the role of music and liturgy to help us unlock emotional blockage?

3. Can musical styles be mixed in the same service, with traditional and contemporary coexisting comfortably?

4. How can people who have gifts to offer be included in ways that make them feel valued and affirmed while the needs of the entire worshiping congregation are served?

What Is Appropriate Music for Worship?

The easiest way around any of these questions is to wrap ourselves in the cloak of "standards." Do we have standards, beliefs? If we believe in nothing, stand for nothing, and remain afraid to articulate our beliefs, we are, in my opinion, always going to be on the run, liturgically and musically. The question is, how do we minister to, affirm, and value those with different tastes? The Very Reverend Pete Gomes, in an AGO address, has this to say about taste:

Part of the problem of taste has not so much to do with the intrinsic worth of the music itself, but rather with the arrogance that so frequently accompanies a fixed notion of what is "right." Taste that breeds arrogance and an exclusivity of aesthetic expression comes perilously close to a violation of the commandment against idolatry and other gods. Such taste, unleavened by tolerance may even be a rebuke to the worship of God. How do we reconcile then the tension between our desire to sing the Lord's song in the best possible way, and our knowledge that the Lord's song may both be sung and heard in ways foreign and even distasteful to us. [6]

Perhaps some light on what is "appropriate" might come as we look at new hymnals coming out in these last years. Here is an opportunity to find out what is deemed appropriate. The new *United Methodist Hymnal*, for example, is a good and useful book, reflecting great diversity and offering a resource broad in its scope. Yes, we'll have "In the Garden" and "Onward, Christian Soldiers," and "The Battle Hymn of the Republic" because ours was an open process that elicited response from across the denomination. We have not sold out to any one concern, but have attempted to balance as many needs as possible in a book not too heavy to be carried by one able-bodied person. Many traditions have been preserved, while allowing the Lord's song to be sung in new and different ways. Perhaps this "balance" is a partial answer to the entire question of what is "appropriate." New occasions do teach new duties. Certainly what is appropriate has a lot to do with what is chosen, why, and how it is presented. This leads to the second question.

What Is the Function of Music and Liturgy?

Here, we are speaking about the "practice" of church music, or its function. Erik Routley brings words of wisdom:

> Everything seems to depend on what is meant by worship function. If the function of worship is to let people know that they're "OK" and not in too much need of reconstruction, then the practice of church music serves that quite adequately. If its intention is to stretch them, then I would have my doubts. But it will always be like this and visionaries mustn't lose their compassion.[7]

"What we have in common with Great Britain," says Routley, "is a temptation to let standards down in the name of a contemptible doctrine that good taste is the enemy of charity." [8]

Dr. Robert Baker often remarked that the church should not have to choose between a "dedicated dud" or a "proficient pagan." When we speak of "cerebral" versus "emotional," the issue of excellence in the music or liturgy surfaces. Does it matter if anything is done well in a worship service? Do those who attend really bring different eyes than those they brought to the ballet, different ears than when they attended the symphony, different tastes and sensibilities? Do they, as Robert Shaw once suggested, hang their brains alongside their hats as they enter church?

And what of ministry? John Wilson, church musician, composer, and arranger believes that much more is needed than musical excellence. He believes that worship can be effective without it if that commodity is not within one's grasp. "Too many directors are so preoccupied with achieving high musical standards and impressing their contemporaries, that they forget what their primary responsibilities are . . . to glorify God and to lead their people into a true worship experience." [9]

So, Benji, here's the question within the question. Do we choose music for worship that is easily accessible to both singer and listener, sing it with prerecorded tape, so that the pleasant texts and harmonies move the congregation to respond? Do we shy away from anything "learned" or "traditional"? Is participation our goal? Are 300 singers twice as powerful as 150? Is the music of the "masters" actually suspect in this context?

There is no easy answer, of course, but I believe it is possible, with judicious choice, careful balancing of elements, and an inviting posture to combine both the cerebral and the emotional in the same service. I believe that one need not sacrifice "ministry" in the name of standards, or "standards" in the name of ministry. That tension is the name of the game. We are in ministry when we choose well and execute properly. The third question deals with this balance of differing styles.

Bach and Rock in the Same Service?

If worship is to survive, we will find opportunity to use as many different expressions of music, liturgy, banners, and dance, as we find appropriate places. We are called to be wise, pastoral, educational, humorous, and tolerant. It may be that the polarization of a "contemporary service" or a "traditional service" or a "folk service" gives out a misleading signal. Differing styles ought to be able to coexist comfortably together. If we are not comfortable or capable in every style, we can find persons who are and who will present these gifts with style and integrity.

In this regard, it is essential that pastor and musician communicate what they know about the service to each other. Which scripture is to be used for the sermon is often not enough. A paragraph expressing where he or she hopes to go with the scripture is so very helpful. Musicians need to be sensitive to pastors when something extraordinary is going on with the music—from change in physical setup to length. So many battles need not be fought if communication is constant.

A major complaint voiced by musicians across the country is that they never know what their pastors are going to preach until it is too late to coordinate, to find the right anthem, psalm, prelude, or hymn! The pastors would doubtless like it if musicians were a bit more flexible and creative in their choice and use of music and/or instruments. We musicians sometimes are the "War Department" and do not help the cause. I believe that worshipers perceive a oneness in a service, consciously or unconsciously and recognize appropriate choice and smooth flow.

I also believe that the Holy Spirit works best alongside of us. An unplanned service, depending on the offices of the Holy Spirit can be an affront to the Almighty. I've heard many sermons, and several preludes and anthems, whose obvious dependence on this heavenly helper reminds one of the school child who, not having studied, prays for a good grade on the test. I once heard a soloist give a lengthy and moving introduction to his song, giving the Holy Spirit credit for "leading" him to sing it. After a bad presentation, in which he lost his place several times, a lady sitting across from me said, "Isn't it wonderful that the Lord 'led' that man to sing that song?" I responded, rather uncharitably, "Too bad the Lord didn't lead him to learn it."

Does this singer need affirmation as a person? Certainly! What about his gift of song? Well, I would never encourage rudeness, but I would expect preparation. This is the heart of the fourth question.

How Can Those with Gifts Be Affirmed
in Ways that Serve the Whole Body?

How do we affirm the giver without having blindly to accept and use the gift? What we can hope to do is to attempt to value and affirm the giver, knowing that he or she almost always wants me to value, love, and accept the gift as well, and usually is not very subtle about it. We can find opportunities for use of the gift in appropriate settings. And, we can expect from everyone—pastor, musician, and congregation alike—an attitude of hospitality. Remember Dr. Palmer's statement about hospitality: Hospitality doesn't make learning painless, but makes painful things possible.

I believe, you see, that we have responsibility to lead in love, but not be run over. Some of the most rude, critical behavior you will encounter exhibits itself in church settings. When that congregational member, with piercing look and mad countenance pounces upon you with the question: "Can the organist play *softer*?" I have an answer: "Yes!" Nothing more. You are not going to win that argument and a simple answer pulls the plug on an unpleasant situation.

I believe we are called to love, but not to be doormats. We are called to understand that a church is where you come when you're *not* OK, and you are embraced, cared for, encouraged, stretched, and made part of the community. Whether the service has included Bach or Brubeck, Grechaninov or Grant (Amy, that is), Gallus or Gaither, you have been touched and, in part, made whole by the community experience. As they say in the books, that's OK!

Notes

1. William Easum, *Dancing with Dinosaurs: Ministry in a Hostile and Hurting Church* (Nashville: Abingdon Press, 1993), p. 84.

2. John Bisagno, quoted in ibid, p. 85.

3. Easum, *Dancing with Dinosaurs,* p. 84.

4. Paul Westermeyer, *The American Organist* (November 1993): 36.

5. Ibid.

6. Peter Gomes, *The American Organist* (April 1981): 31.

7. Erik Routley, *Church Music* (Concordia, 1976): 2.

8. Ibid.

9. John Wilson, *Church Music* (Concordia, 1976): 4-5.